Urban Photography
Using
Small Digital Cameras

Jeff Stefan

Table of Contents

Urban Photography: A Way of Life

Before I became a full time photographer and videographer, I wandered the streets of Detroit during lunch taking photographs. I was lucky enough to work downtown and it was the highpoint of my day. I carried a couple of small, inexpensive point-and-shoot digital cameras, and occasionally a full frame DSLR (Digital Single Lens Reflex). When I got back from lunch I checked the images out on the camera LCD displays. Sometimes I got some good shots, sometimes not. It depended on the situations, weather and people I encountered on my walks. Even if I came away with nothing, at least I was *out there shooting*. I was itching to get home and upload the shots to my computer and process them. Most of all, I was looking forward to the next day's lunchtime shoot. I also took advantage of any free time I had and went shooting whenever I visited another city.

During these shoots I realized how easily urban and street photography could become a way of life for a photographer.

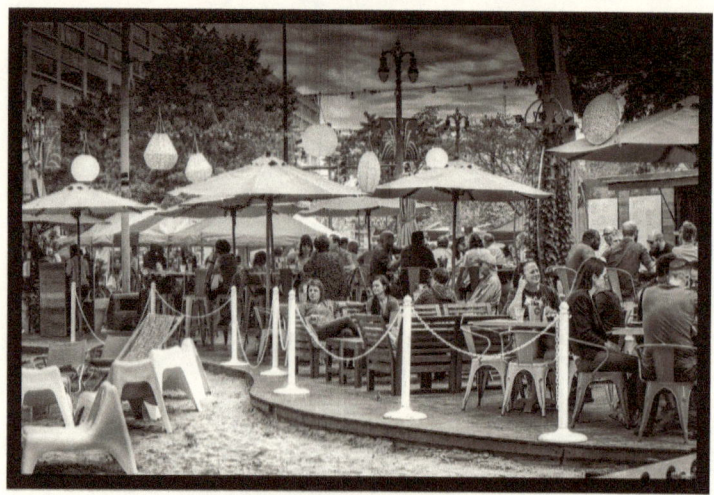

Campus Martius, downtown Detroit, Michigan
Canon 5D Mark III f/8 at 1/125 ISO 100

Urban environments constantly change- people, attitudes, fashions, buildings, storefronts, you name it. It's always dynamic, which is one of the great enticements of urban photography. There is always something unusual and interesting to photograph in the most obscure nooks and crannies of a city or town, if you take the time to look.

The shot below was taken in late September when the sun was low on the horizon, producing the interesting reflections on the pavement. The man crouching with his phone made for a good subject and focal point. I was lucky to come across this scene and shoot it.

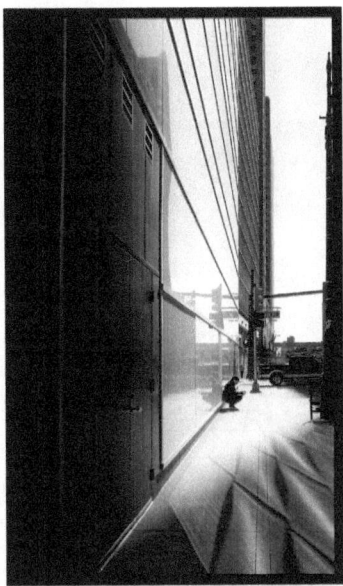

Man Texting, downtown Detroit
Nikon S3100 f/3.4 at 1/800 ISO 400

Street Photography: The Beginning

Shooting on the streets dates back to the infancy of photography, and emerged with a few historically significant photographers, Paul Strand and Alfred Stieglitz being two of them. Check out their classic photographs **Wall Street** and **Winter, Fifth Avenue** as examples. Instead of posed portraits or documentary type architectural photographs, they captured the energy and life of the streets of their time with outstanding, spontaneous compositions. Their photographs made real statements.

Pure street photography is all about timing and capturing people in moments and situations that will never exist again. Urban photography is wider in scope, where you still have the spontaneity of shooting people on the street, but you can take a little more time looking for and composing environmental and cultural shots. Both are certainly not leisurely activities- you have to be ready to instantaneously shoot whatever is revealed to you at any moment.

Urban and Street Photography: Joined at the Hip

So what's the difference between urban and street photography? Not much, but for me, urban photography goes beyond candid shots of people on the street. It also comprehends the environment, the time and the culture of the location where the shots are taken.

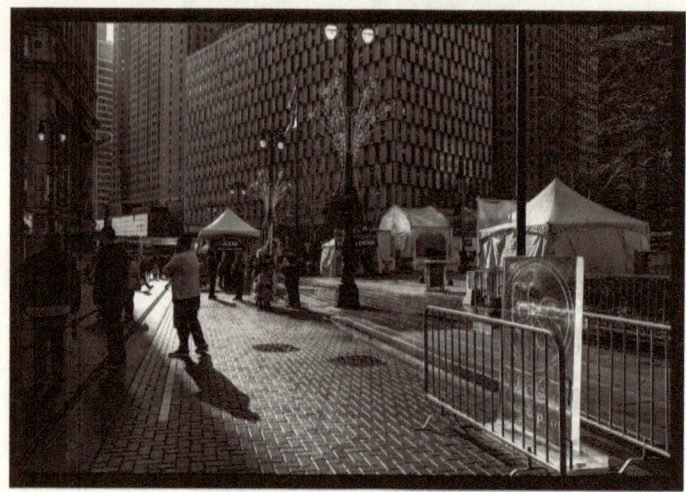

Campus Martius, Detroit, Michigan
Canon 5D Mark III f/6.3 at 1/1000 ISO 400

Most street photographers are known for their people and faces. Look at Bruce Gilden or Garry Winograd's work. They shoot mostly people, close up (especially Bruce Gilden). Others, such as Robert Frank and Vivian Maier considered the environment people existed in and conveyed that with insight and meaning. In this book we're lumping the two schools of practice together.

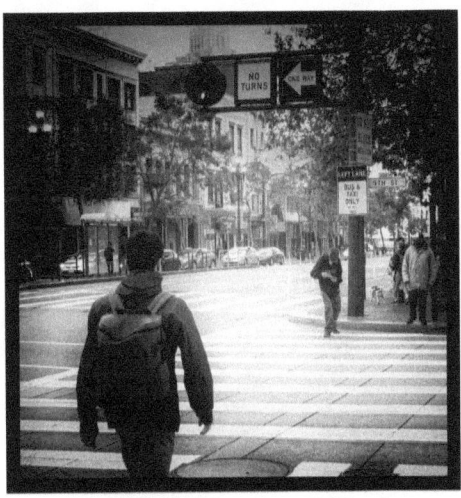

9th Street, San Francisco, California
Canon S110 f/4 at 1/800 ISO 2000

My working definition of urban photography is **capturing the people, environment and culture of our time.**

Black and White vs. Color

As far as I'm concerned, urban and street photography is less effective unless the images are in black and white. To me, a color urban image defies this grand tradition and lacks the timeless impact of black and white. Look at the wonderful images of Henri Cartier-Bresson. If you look at photographs like *Hyères, 1932* or *Cell in a Model Prison in the U.S.A., 1975,* it's hard to imagine them being effective in color. The only real exceptions I can think of is the work of Fred Herzog, and maybe Joel Meyerowitz. If you've never heard of them, please check out their work.

That doesn't mean you have to shoot digitally in black and white. It's best to shoot in color and de-saturate your images when you post process them. We will cover that later in this book. Remember, this is just my opinion. If you love shooting in color, by all means, do. Shoot what's in your heart and mind and develop your own style.

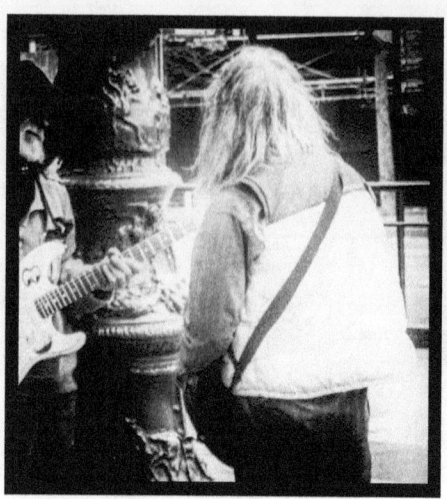

Guitar Player, San Francisco, California
Canon S110 f/5.6 at 1/800 ISO 2000

Cameras: Film vs. Digital

Urban and street photography got its real start in the 1920s with the emergence of 35mm film and small rangefinder cameras with viewfinders. Henri Cartier-Bresson burst on the scene in the 1930s and was a master of "the decisive moment". Cartier-Bresson used a Leica rangefinder and a 50mm lens, supposedly never cropped his images outside the camera and never used flash. If I were forced to rank urban photographers, I would rank Henri Cartier-Bresson as number one based on his trailblazing work. For me, Robert Frank, Diane Arbus and Vivian Maier follow right behind.

There's a traditional gold standard camera series for film street photography, and those are the Leica M 35mm film rangefinders. Many, many photographers still use these cameras today. They are reliable, durable and their lenses are incomparable to others rangefinders. Many believe the Leica M3 was the best built camera of all time. Another great feature of the M3 is that that body is backward compatible with 70 year old lenses, or so I'm told. Cartier-Bresson used an M3. So did Robert Frank and countless others.

The older SLRs (Single Lens Reflex) film cameras are also good for urban photography, although they aren't really true to the rangefinder tradition. Older SLRs such as the Canon F1 or Nikon F2 are great film cameras, top of the line in their day and perform well on the street. I still shoot film with a Canon F1. It's build as solid as a tank and is small compared to today's DSLRs. So is the Nikon F2. Vintage Nikon lenses, ones the fit the F2, are incredibly sharp. Compared to bulky DSLRs, these two SLRs seem like half the size, which is an advantage when out shooting in the field.

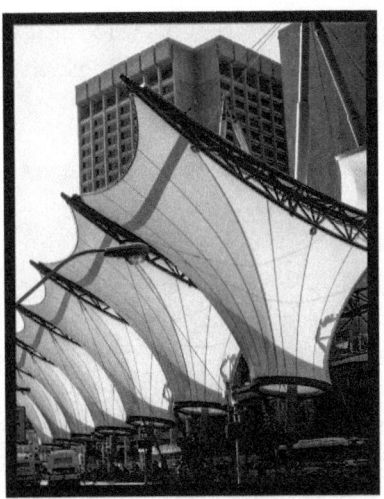

Greyhound Bus Station, Detroit, Michigan
Canon S110 f/6.3 at 1/1250 ISO 400

Not all trailblazing urban photographers shot with 35mm film. Two noted photographers mentioned before shot with 6x6cm Twin Lens Reflex Rolleflex cameras: Diane Arbus and Vivian Maier. Both were phenomenal urban photographers and their images are as compelling today as when they were first taken.

Cameras Used In This Book

So much for history. We are in a digital age, and although film photography is surging, urban photography lends itself well to small digital cameras, point-and-shoots in particular. Almost all of the photographs in this book were taken with inexpensive digital point-and-shoots. One is a Canon PowerShot S110, another is a Canon G12, and another is a Nikon Coolpix S3100. These are inexpensive, durable and reliable cameras. I chose the Nikon Coolpix S3100 as an example camera in this book because it is so simple to use and is dirt cheap. I got some of my favorite shots with this camera over the years. It finally broke and I replaced it with an S3600, which is essentially the same inexpensive camera.

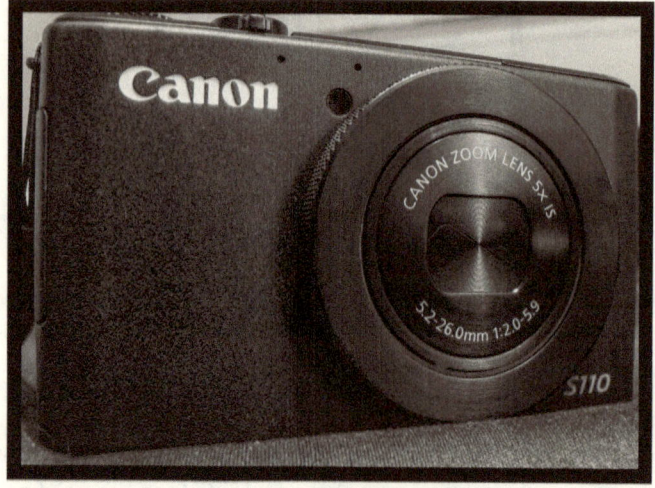

Canon S110

All three cameras are no longer made but are available used. As of this writing, the Canon S110 goes from $150-200, a G12 goes for around $200 and a Nikon S3100 goes for as little as $20. **Any small point and shoot will work well, from the simplest to the most expensive.** The key is being small, fast and easy to operate.

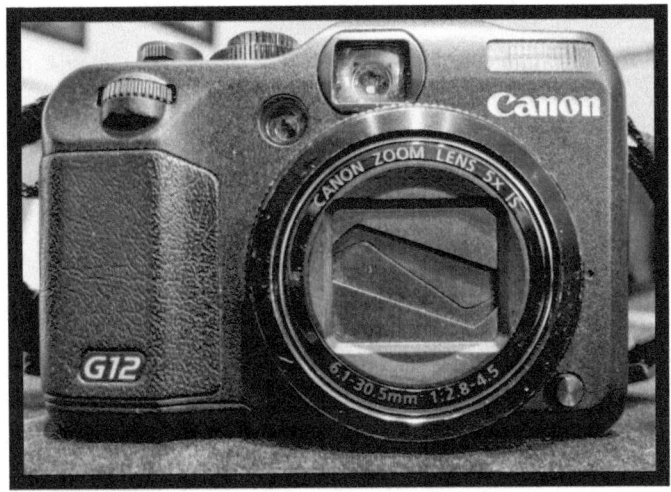

Canon G12

As you can see, my G12 is pretty beaten up, but it still works just fine. These point-and-shoot cameras are covered in detail in an earlier book, **Exploiting Your Point and Shoot.** Some chapters will be reiterated here to keep important and relevant information in one place.

Point and shoot cameras are often overlooked as serious cameras. They should not be, and they're really useful for urban photography. Why? First, they're small and stealthy, second, more advanced point-and-shoots offer a lot of useful DSLR-like features.

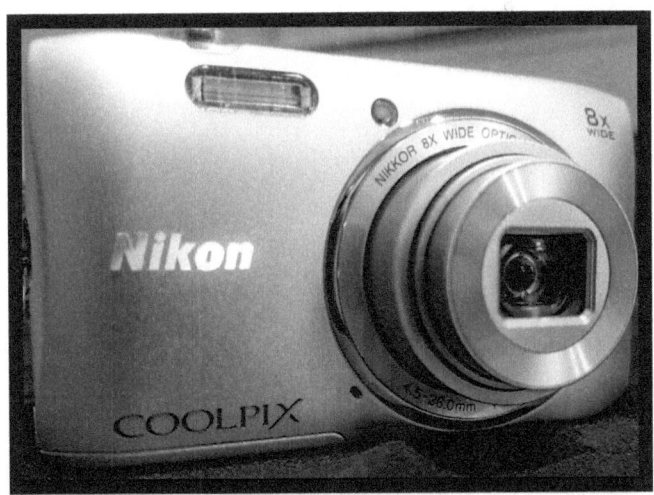

Nikon Coolpix S3600

They are humble cameras, to be sure, but their price, performance and durability make them great urban photography cameras.

A few of the shots in this book were taken with a DSLR (Digital Single Lens Reflex) camera, namely a Canon 5D Mark III and a few with a Canon T2i. One image was taken with an iPhone. Large, expensive full frame DSLRs such as the 5D Mark III are not the preferred tools used in this book. Carrying around a bulky DSLR with a big lens and pointing it at people at close range is not a good way to get effective urban shots. That's why the smaller point-and-shoots work so well. People hardly see them.

So what about smart phones? They are fine, but they have issues regarding manual exposure control, ISO, white balance and depth of field. Most cell phone cameras have an infinite depth of field, which means that everything is in focus, making it difficult or impossible to focus on a subject and have the background blurry.

What You Will Learn

This books is short and does not contain any fluff. You will:

Learn the basics of digital photography

It's important to know your camera inside and out when shooting in the street. There should be no guesswork or fiddling around with camera settings you're unsure of while shooting. It's all about capturing the best fleeting moments and the camera should be an extension of you. You must master your tools.

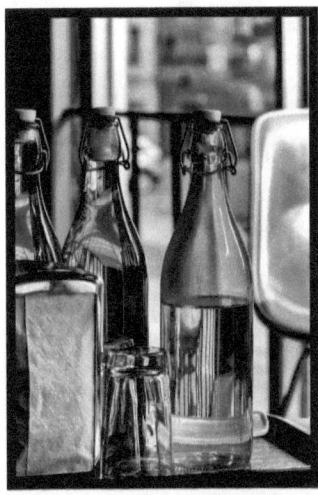

Urban Bean Company, Detroit
Canon T2i f/8 at 1/100 ISO 200

Learn how to compose effective shots out in the streets

Composition rules do not go out the window when shooting on the streets. Composition concepts like leading lines and negative space still apply. To get great street shots, you need these concepts to be internalized and automatic.

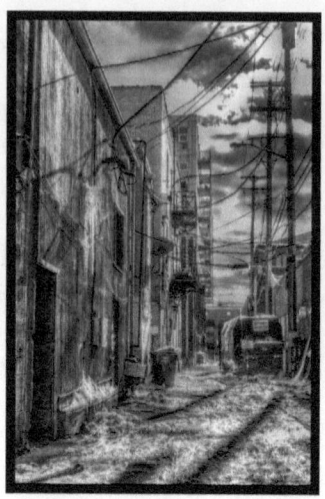

Alley, Royal Oak, Michigan
Canon S110 f/16 at 1/500 ISO 1500

Learn how to position yourself to get cool street shots

Do you plant yourself at a location and wait for things to happen, or do you walk the streets looking for shots? Both have their advantages and disadvantages, and both are covered in this book.

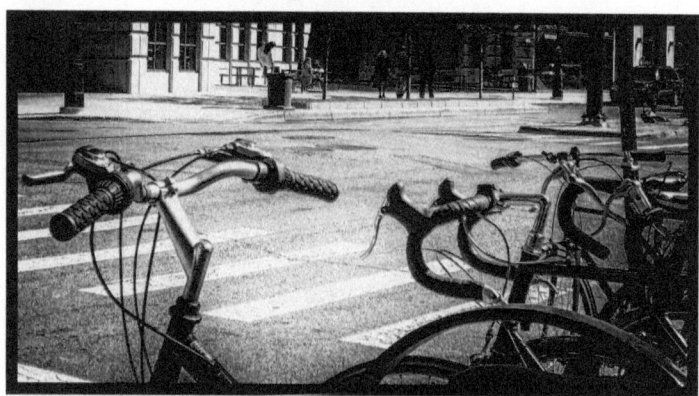

Bikes, Detroit
Nikon S3100 f/4.5 at 1/500 ISO 80

Get over the fear of being seen and approached

Are you nervous about shooting on the street and worried about someone getting in your face? Can you make yourself inconspicuous while getting great shots? What do you say if someone comes up to you? These situations are considered and there are ways to make yourself almost "invisible".

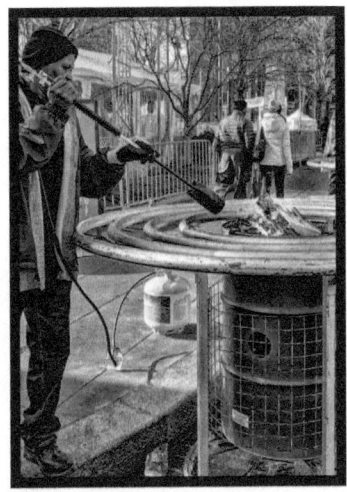

Campus Martius, Detroit
Canon 5D Mark III f/11 at 1/160 ISO 400

Learn about subject and theme in your street shots

Subject and theme are two essential elements of great urban photography. Your images need to *say something.*

Taking and Keeping Notes

I've included five blank pages for notes at the end of this book. Why? I believe it's important not only to shoot on the streets but to take notes. What kind of day was it? What compelled you to pick your shooting location or subjects? What are you trying to express? It's a great habit to get into, and years down the line you will reflect on your early notes with affection. I wish I was a better note taker over the years. Whenever I come across some rare old notes, it takes me right back to that shoot.

Toss this book in your camera bag on your first few outings and try and jot down a few notes. Trust me, you will be thankful you did a few years down the line.

Digital Photography Basics

Most of this text appeared in the book **Exploiting Your Point and Shoot** but is included here for reference and completeness.

Before diving into shooting urban environments, read this section to familiarize yourself with terms and features that are common to digital photography and digital cameras. If you've just started reading this book and find this section boring, move on to the other chapters.

Once you want to know more about how digital cameras work, come back here because it's important to know this stuff. It's unlikely that you will become a proficient photographer and advance your skills without understanding these basics. Again, you must master your tools.

Image Sensors

Image sensors are the heart of any digital camera, from the most expensive full frame DSLR to the cheapest point-and-shoot. Image sensors are the digital equivalent of film. Image sensors are filled with millions of little holes that basically convert light into electrons. After the conversion, each cell contains an electrical charge. The accumulated charge for each cell is read and converted into a digital value. From these digital values images are recorded.

There are generally two types of image sensors, CCDs (Charge Couple Devices) and CMOS (Complementary Metal Oxide Semiconductors). CCD sensors are more expensive but provide lower noise and higher quality images. This is the exception and not the rule, especially with respect to the expensive part. An inexpensive Nikon Coolpix S3100 (or 3600) sports a 1/2.3-in CCD image sensor at 20.1 megapixels. A Canon PowerShot S110 contains a 1/1.7 CMOS sensor at 12.1 megapixels and costs over twice as much as a Coolpix S3600.

Exposure

Exposure determines the amount and duration of light allowed to fall on the image sensor. Exposure is adjustable via aperture and shutter speed settings. The sensitivity of the image sensor is adjusted through the ISO settings.

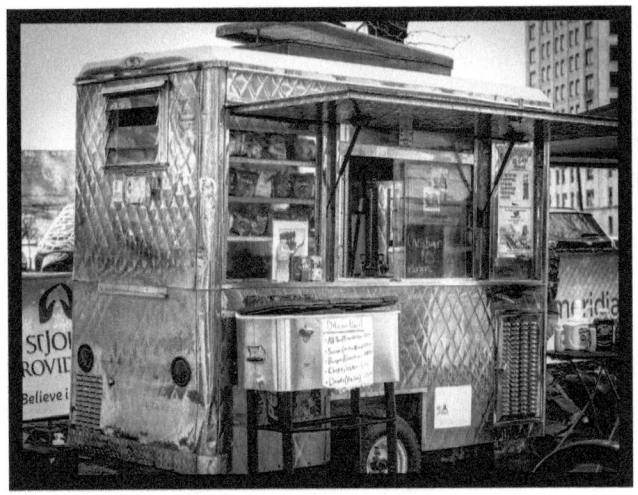

Food Trailer, Detroit
Canon S110 f/4 at 1/800 ISO 2000

Aperture

Aperture is how **much** light a lens allows to fall on the image sensor. Aperture is measured in f-stops. The lower the f-stop the more light enters the lens, which means the lens glass and coatings are generally or higher quality, making the lens (and therefore the camera) more expensive.

Point-and-shoots have zoom lenses and many people don't pay attention to the aperture values. You should, though, when selecting a camera. On a Canon PowerShot S110 the lowest f-stop is f/2.0, which is decent. This is only at the full wide-angle focal length. When the lens is zoomed in it quickly degrades to f/5.9 as it approaches full telephoto length. The Nikon Coolpix S3100 is at f/3.7 at wide angle and f/6.6 at telephoto length. Go by this rule of thumb; the lower the f-stop a camera supports when zoomed in, the better the lens.

Why the term f-stop? The f stands for focal ratio. Each f-stop allows in twice as much (or twice as little) light as the f-stop next to it. F-stops generally scale from 1, 2, 4, 8 16, etc. F-stops, at first glance, seem backwards. F11 is a larger number than F2.0, so you would think F11 would let more light through the lens. The opposite is true. The greater the f-stop value, the less light is allowed through the lens.

For more inexpensive point-and-shoots such as the Coolpix S3100 or S3600, there is no direct aperture control. You may think that you can change the f-stop setting by fiddling with ISO and exposure compensation, but you won't. The shutter speed will change and not the aperture value. So are you stuck? Not really. F-stops on this type of point-and-shoot are controlled by the current focal length of the zoom lens. If you slightly zoom in on a subject the f-stop value will increase, allowing less light through the lens. If you zoom out, the f-stop value will decrease, allowing more light through the lens.

It's a different story with more feature laden point-and-shoots such as the Canon PowerShot S110 or G12. Aperture can be controlled directly in Av (Aperture value) mode. This is also referred to as Aperture Priority mode, so consider the terms interchangeable. Same with the shutter speed in Tv (Time value) mode. This is more commonly referred to as Shutter Priority mode. These and other modes are detailed a little later.

Shutter Speed

If aperture controls how much light hits your camera sensor, shutter speed controls how **long** light sits on the sensor. The shutter speed works like an f-stop. It either doubles or halves the amount of light hitting the sensor by keeping the sensor exposed to light for a longer or shorter period of time.
Shutter speed values are expressed in reciprocal seconds. For example, a shutter speed of 1/15 means that the image sensor will be exposed to light for 0.066 seconds. On a simple point-and-shoot like the S3100 you can control the shutter speed by changing ISO values.

Why is it when you change one thing, like ISO, the shutter speed or f-stop setting changes? It's called *reciprocity*. ISO, aperture and shutter speed are all related. It makes sense that if you have a properly metered exposure and the aperture is adjusted to a different f-stop to let in twice the amount of light, the shutter speed must be increased to allow half as much light as previously allowed to enter. That keeps all things equal. If you change the ISO to make the image sensor more or less sensitive to light, the aperture and/or shutter speed must be adjusted to keep the exposure the same. This doesn't matter all that much with really inexpensive point-and-shoots like the Nikon S3100 but makes a big difference applied to more capable cameras.

Exposure Revisited

Digital cameras, including point-and-shoots, evaluate exposure via different metering modes. The metering modes measure light to calculate a correct exposure. Understanding and utilizing these modes in different lighting situations can turn a good shot into a great one. There are three primary metering modes, *evaluative, center weighted average* and *spot*.

Evaluative Metering

This is the default mode on most cameras. The camera evaluates the subject brightness and background and tries to determine the best overall exposure. Evaluative metering does not do well in high contrast situations. Chances are, if your subject is strongly backlit the subject will be slightly underexposed and dark.

Center Weighted Average Metering

This metering mode is used by many portrait photographers. Center weighted average metering evaluates the average brightness across the whole image area but weighs the central area more heavily. You may or may not find this mode useful.

Spot Metering

Spot metering tightens even further around the center of the viewing or focus area. This allows for almost pinpoint exposure control around a subject. The space and objects around the correctly metered subject may be under or over exposed.

Think as exposure control as a hose. Evaluative metering looks at all the light and is like a fire hose. Center weighted average is like a garden hose with some light spraying out on the sides and spot metering is like a straw.

Here's a drawing showing how light hits your sensor in each metering mode.

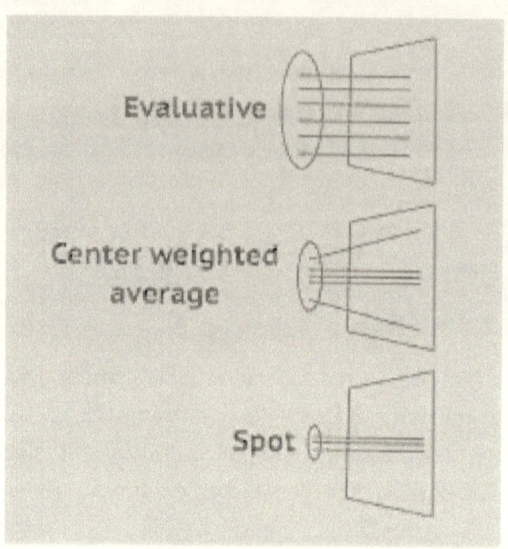

Exposure Compensation

Exposure compensation is available on most point-and-shoots, even on an inexpensive camera like the Coolpix S3100 or S3600. I use exposure compensation a lot, and have it assigned to the control ring on the Canon PowerShot S110. I usually underexpose most shots by one stop or less. Why? To me, it brings out more drama in a photograph.

Check your camera manual for the exposure compensation control and experiment with it. It's usually very accessible which makes it convenient for use. For example, on the Coolpix S3100 exposure compensation is a fixed function on the multi-selector.

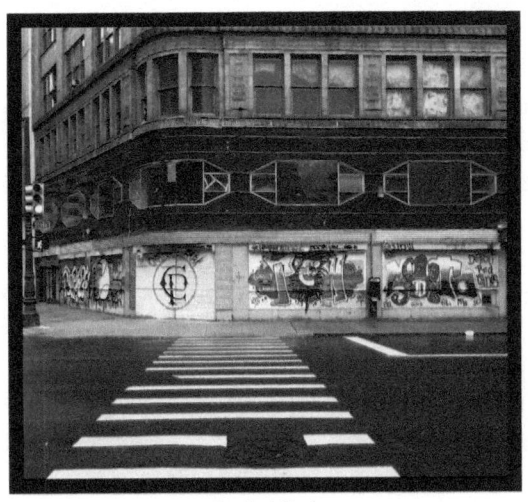

Capitol Park
Nikon S3100 f/3.2 at 1/125 ISO 2000

Using the Histogram

If your point-and-shoot supports a histogram, learn to use it and rely on it. It's really the only way to know if your exposure is correct, and will show you at a glance if there are extreme blacks and whites. For some reason histograms put many photographers off, thinking they are too complicated to understand. That's what I thought initially, but nothing could be further from the truth. Histograms provide exposure information laid out on an X (horizontal) and Y (vertical) axis. The horizontal X axis is measured in units of brightness, with pure black on the extreme left and pure white on the extreme right. The vertical Y axis is measured in pixel units.

Depth of field

Depth of field, or DOF, is what is in focus in front of and behind your subject. DOF is primarily controlled by aperture setting or f-stop. A lower number f-stop, such as f/2.1 will have a shallow DOF, meaning a smaller area will be in focus. On a low end point-and-shoot like the S3600, depth of field is difficult to manage since you don't have direct control over the aperture value. It's kind of like a smart phone in this respect. On a more expensive point-and-shoot such as the PowerShot S110 or PowerShot G12 it's easy to change in in Manual, Av (Aperture priority) or Tv (Time value) modes.

Digital vs. Optical Zoom

Optical zoom uses the physical lens to make your image appear closer. Digital zoom electronically enlarges the image. Optical zoom is superior to digital zoom. Many photographers disable digital zoom on their point-and-shoots and perform any extra enlargement during post processing. This is a good practice.

Most point-and-shoots let you know when the optical zoom maximum is reached. I tend not to exceed the optical zoom maximum, if I use it at all. Digital zoom is automatically disabled on the PowerShot S110 when shooting in RAW mode (RAW is explained later).

ISO or "Film Speed"

I put "film speed" in quotes, since, of course, digital cameras don't use film. They do use ISO ratings, though. ISO stands for International Standards Organization. The higher the ISO number, the more sensitive the image sensor is to light. The lower the ISO number, the less sensitive your image sensor is to light. Most point-and-shoots allow you to increase or decrease ISO settings. Ideally during the day an ISO of 100 to 400 is good. In low light situations the ISO number needs to be cranked up. A high ISO value has a side effect, called noise. The more noise in an image the grainier it will appear. Sometimes, though, a lot of noise or grain helps a photograph, especially in urban photography.

Experiment around with ISO settings on your point-and-shoot. This will help you understand the you're camera's performance and find a range of ISO settings you prefer in different lighting conditions.

White Balance

So what in the world is white balance? You, as a human being, see white one way and your point-and-shoot, as a light processing machine, sees it another. Colors are balanced offsets from what the camera considers white. Think of white as neutral, where every other color is offset from the neutral color. White under sunlight is very different than white under an tungsten light bulb. It's all based on color temperature or CT, which is measured in degrees Kelvin. Daylight is typically at 5200 degrees Kelvin or 5200K. Color temperature is all about the *hue* of the light source. Daylight (5200K) has a different CT than tungsten light (3200K). If your point-and-shoot lets you control white balance and you set the white balance to tungsten and shoot in daylight, your shot will have a distinct bluish cast. Even inexpensive point-and-shoots like the Coolpix S3100 give you control over white balance, as well as more expensive cameras like the PowerShot S110 and Canon G-series cameras. Same goes for Leica, Olympus, Panasonic and the other point-and-shoots. Usually auto white balance works quite well.

You can manipulate white balance to your advantage in certain shooting situations if you're looking for a particular mood for your shots, assuming you're shooting in color. If you want a cold, somewhat bleak look and are shooting outdoors set your white balance to tungsten. If you want an extra warm look inside under tungsten lighting, set your white balance to daylight. The higher the color temperature, the warmer your image will appear.

Memory Cards

Memory cards come in two basic types: compact flash (CF) and SDHC. SDHC stands for Secure Digital High Capacity. Compact flash cards are used on higher quality DSLRs so we won't discuss them here. Most SD cards range from 4GB to 128GB. SDXC cards are used to capture high definition video. So, what card to get? Depending on how you intend to shoot, look for speed and not just capacity. Avoid cheap cards- they will only cause you problems.

If you want to dive into street or sports photography, the faster the image sensor can write data to the SD card translates directly into the time it takes for your camera to set itself up for the next shot. Few things are more frustrating than seeing a shot opportunity and can't take advantage of it because you have to wait for your camera to recycle. I've missed a lot of shots this way where I shouldn't have. Fast-writing SD cards will be more expensive, but they're worth it.

Why is this so? Your camera contains a memory buffer that saves the image you just shot, and the data is transferred to the SD card. How quickly the memory buffer empties is controlled by the speed of the SD card. The hose analogy works here also. Think of the SD card speed as a hose between the memory buffer and the SD card. The wider diameter the hose, the higher volume of data is transferred. SD card technical advances occur frequently so search the web for reviews of fast SD cards, and when you buy, go with a name brand.

As an aside, I once bought a cheap compact flash card for one of my DSLRs and on just about every first shot I got a memory failure. I not only missed shots but I had to turn the camera on and off again, wait for it to reboot and reformat the card and hope for the best. I replaced it with a more expensive, name brand card and have not had the problem since.

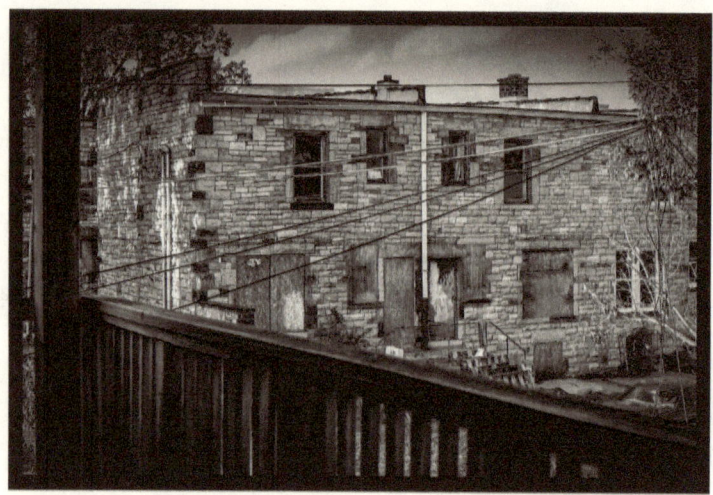

Hostel Detroit Porch, Corktown, Detroit
Nikon Coolpix S3600 f/6 at 1/60 ISO 400

Professional photographers do a couple of things with their memory cards that most people don't. First, they format their memory cards before they go shooting. This removes all images from the card and freshly prepares it to accept new image data. Second, after a shooting session, a lot of pros do not erase their images. Many pros label and file the cards away after the images are transferred to external storage, such as a computer or external hard drive. This is like archiving negatives in the film world. You need to weigh the cost of a memory card vs. the value of the images. For example, of you have a card full of great street shots and are producing a photo essay, you will certainly want to preserve your memory card. Why?

- Your computer might crash, losing transferred images.

- Your external storage device might do the same thing.

- Over time, the people paying for the images may lose them and want to order extras, even years after you've removed them from storage.

Your images are irreplaceable and usually can't be reproduced, especially after long periods of time. It's up to you to weigh the cost.

This method of long-term storage is slowly being replaced by archiving images in the cloud, but you may not always have an internet connection available.

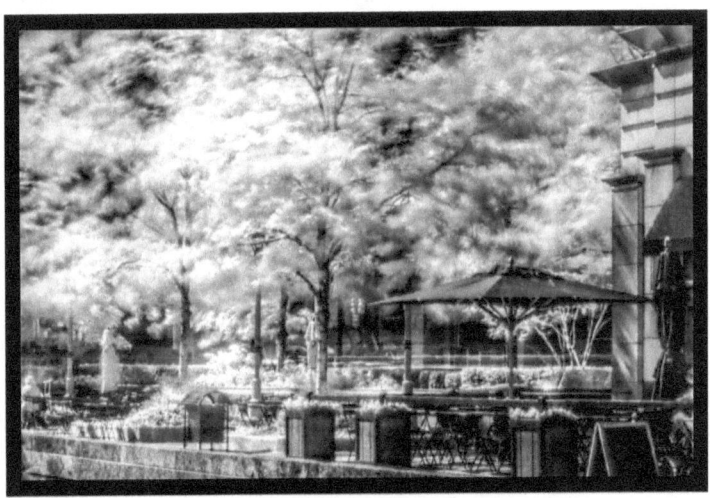

Campus Martius, Detroit, Michigan
Canon T2i f/5.6 at 1/15 ISO 400 with infrared filter

RAW vs. JPEG

RAW files are not images, but raw data from your point-and-shoot's image sensor. That's why it's called "RAW". Processing RAW data requires special software to manipulate, but most image processing applications are now accepting RAW input. Lightroom, GIMP and Pixelmator all support RAW data. In addition, software is usually available from your camera manufacturer's website that enables you to import and process RAW data.

Why shoot in RAW mode? RAW gives you complete control over your image since the data has not been processed, compressed or adulterated. For example, if you are shooting in JPEG mode and the white balance is set incorrectly, you will not be able to color correct your photographs with much success. Say that you set the white balance to tungsten while shooting indoors the night before and now you're shooting in daylight. All of your images will be tinted blue. This is not a problem when shooting in RAW mode, since you can simply change the white balance before you convert them to JPEGs or other formats in your image processing software.

In JPEG format, your image is processed to a degree by the camera. The image is also compressed, losing data in the process. This is called 'lossy' compression. You can fit more images in memory using JPEGs, but your post-processing options will be limited. If your point-and-shoot supports RAW files, use it. You will have control over manipulating your images in post-processing without any information loss.

Shooting Modes

In this chapter we'll take a look at the different shooting modes offered by point-and-shoots, starting with Auto mode.

Auto Mode

All point-and-shoots provide Auto mode. Auto mode attempts to take care of everything for you when you take a shot. This is truly "snapshot" mode. Depending on your camera, Auto may be the only available mode to use. My Coolpix S3600 is in fixed Auto mode and I set the color options to black and white. I use exposure compensation to exercise control over the shot I'm going to take and that's it. I'm forced to work within the constraints of this simple camera.

If you have a more expensive point-and-shoot that provides more sophisticated modes, avoid Auto. More and more point-and-shoots are offering DLSR-like functions, which is great news. Even though you can get great images out of a Nikon Coolpix S3100 class camera, it just scratches the surface of what a multi-mode point-and-shoot can do.

Growing out of Auto mode is growing with your camera. Move up in the sequence described below and you will master your point-and-shoot with time and practice.

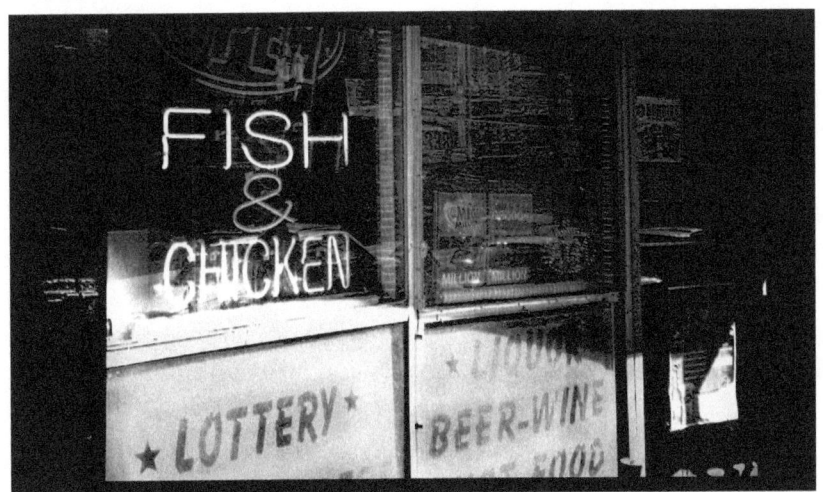

Fish & Chicken, Detroit, Michigan
Nikon Coolpix S3600 f/4.2 at 1/125 ISO 80

P Mode

P mode, or Programmed AE (Auto Exposure) mode is one level up in sophistication from Auto. P mode opens up a wide array of shooting options not available in Auto. I will often shoot in P mode on the Canon PowerShot S110 and use the control ring for exposure compensation. I do the same on the PowerShot G12, especially when street shooting.

So what can you do in P mode over and above Auto? You can set the ISO, metering mode, exposure compensation and white balance. Having the flexibility to change these settings can make or break a shot. Try changing the metering mode to spot and under and overexpose a few shots using exposure compensation. Some of the resulting images will look pretty cool.

If you're shooting on the street make sure your camera is set up and ready to go before hand. Not much is worse than fumbling with camera settings while a shot opportunity passes by. You need to work fast and be ready at all times.

Be mindful of the ISO and white balance settings in P mode since it will heavily influence your exposure. I was out shooting recently with the PowerShot S110 in P mode during the day and set the ISO for 1600 and the white balance for tungsten for some indoor shooting the night before. The images were way overexposed and blue-cast. I didn't have my camera set up and ready to go before I went shooting. You can use auto ISO and white balance, but you gain much more control over your images setting ISO and white balance manually. The sooner you get used to it, the better.

For street photography I like to use spot metering, a higher than normal daylight ISO (around 400) and underexpose the shots a little. It takes some time to find what works, but it's time well spent. This is one baby step in developing your own style.

Work with and understand P mode on your point-and-shoot before moving onto Aperture (Av), Shutter priority (Tv) and Manual modes. What you learn using P mode applies to the other advanced modes.

P mode is almost ideal for urban photography. You can still change the ISO, white balance, exposure compensation and metering mode.

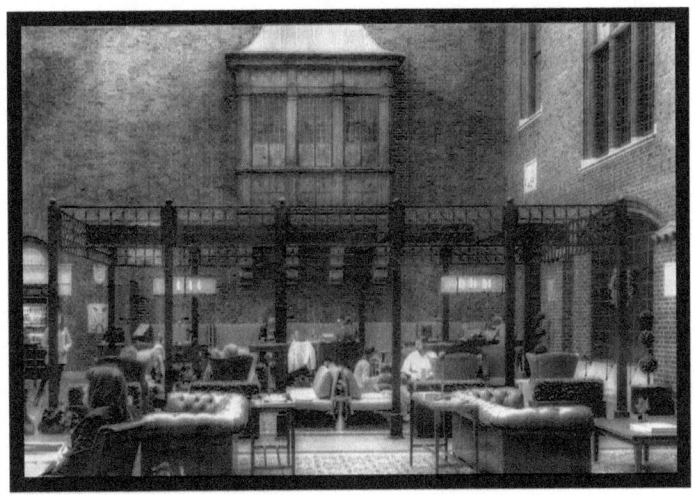

Detroit Institute of Arts
Nikon Coolpix S3100 f/6 at 1/60 ISO 400

Aperture Priority

Once you're comfortable with P mode, move to Aperture priority mode. In this mode you set the aperture (f-stop) value and the camera adjusts the shutter speed to obtain a standard exposure. You still have to be mindful of the ISO and white balance as in P mode. Why Aperture mode? It gives you control of the f-stop settings, which directly effects depth of field and improves shooting in lower light. Remember, the lower the f-stop setting the more light is allowed through the lens and the more shallow the depth of field.

Using a low f-stop setting such as f/2.0 produces a shallow depth of field, which is great if you want to isolate the subject of your photograph since it will limit the focus area. For more depth of field a higher f-stop is better, since more of the frame will be in focus. On Canon cameras Aperture priority mode is marked Av on the control dial. On Nikon cameras it's marked as A. Aperture priority mode is good for urban shots. If you want to isolate individual subjects, including people, a shallow depth of field is the way to go. Your subject will be in focus and the surroundings will not.

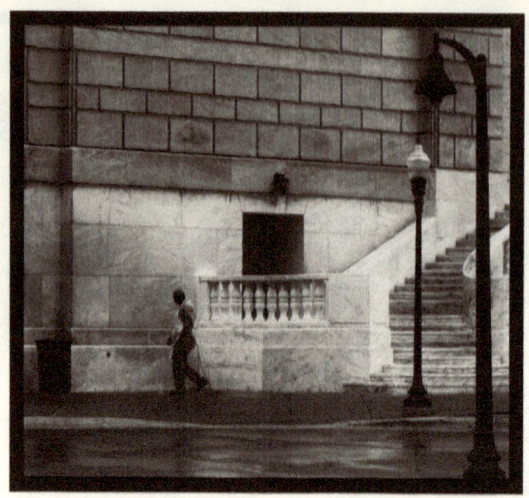

Detroit Institute of Arts
Nikon Coolpix S3600 f/6 at 1/60 ISO 400

Shutter Priority (Time Value)

Shutter priority mode is the opposite of Aperture mode. You set the shutter speed and the camera sets the f-stop to obtain a standard exposure. Why is this useful? The slower the shutter speed means the image sensor is exposed to light for a longer period of time. A slow shutter speed is great for producing flowing motion shots, such as a silky smooth waterfall or headlights streaming on a highway. I have to confess I don't use Shutter priority mode very much and am partial to P mode, Aperture and Manual but I plan on practicing with it.

Street shots taken in shutter priority mode are a gamble, but sometimes you get a shot worth its weight in gold. Using a slow shutter speed and following a subject with your camera is one way to get that great shot. If you're lucky, the subject in motion will be still and focused and the background will be a blur, amplifying them motion. This takes some practice.

Manual

Once you master P, Aperture and Shutter priority modes it's time to move on to the ultimate in control: Manual mode. Manual gives you complete control over aperture and shutter speed settings. This is trickier for street photography but can make for more controlled and dramatic shots. Utilizing manual mode correctly and internalizing it with your camera takes a lot of practice, but it's worth it.

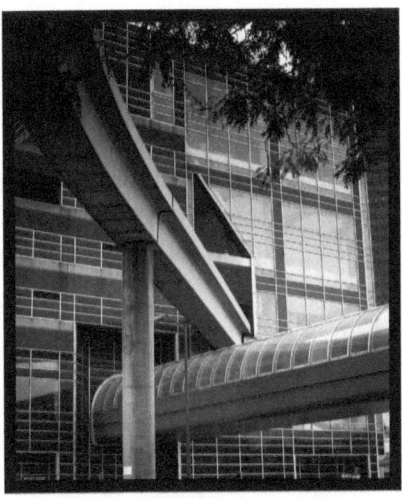

Millender Center, Detroit, Michigan
Nikon Coolpix S3100 f/6 at 1/60 ISO 400

I learned photography using manual, match-needle film cameras which I think is an advantage. Generally, I would set the f-stop where I wanted it and adjust the shutter speed to get a standard exposure. What I really was doing was manually setting the camera to Aperture priority mode. I used the camera's built-in light meter and also used a handheld light meter. When auto exposure cameras first came out, such as the Canon AE-1, I was skeptical-*really* skeptical about turning over control of my exposures. It took a long time for me to trust the different priority modes but cameras are so good these days I don't give it a second thought for most situations.

In Manual you really have to know your camera and be able to make quick exposure decisions without thinking too much. All it takes is getting out on the streets and practice.

Camera Feature Breakdowns

There are basically two types of point and shoots. One type has DSLR-like features, such as exposure modes, aperture and shutter speed controls, and settable ISO and white balance. The Canon S110 and G12 provide these and more controls, where a simple camera such as the Nikon S3100 does not. For urban photography, that's okay and is sometimes an advantage.

We need speed and accurate exposures and don't have time to fiddle with camera settings while out on the streets. I tend to let the camera do most of the work when urban shooting.

Timing is everything when your shooting out on the streets. Letting a great image pass you by while you struggle with camera settings is a cardinal sin of urban photography. In the old press film photography days the old adage was "f/8 and be there." There's a lot to be said for that. Aperture settings such as f/8 and f/11 capture a wide depth of field. If you're shooting in Aperture priority mode on a decently lit day, these settings work great.

Canon PowerShot S110 Setup

When I shoot on the street with the S110 I use AV (aperture priority) and P (programmed automatic) modes. I rely a lot on the camera's automation. If I have a reasonable amount of time to compose an environmental shot, I'll shoot in Manual, otherwise it's P or AV. If I'm shooting in AV mode, I'll set the aperture to f/8 or f/11 and leave it there most of the time. If the situation and lighting is volatile and I need to get a sequence of shots fast, I'll switch to P mode. As I mentioned before, you can also get some great motion shots in Shutter priority mode.

I set the ring function to exposure compensation and the white balance to Auto. I also set the ISO to Auto. Also, I set the image mode to RAW. I bounce around from setting the exposure metering from Evaluative to Spot. That's all I do for street shooting. This camera is much more capable, but these settings work for me and they accommodate most ever changing shooting situations.

As I mentioned, if I'm stationary, have time to set up shots, and the subject has consistent lighting, I'll switch to Manual mode. I've found it effective when stationary to set the exposure mode to spot metering. The most common scenario when staying stationary is to shoot interesting people as they walk by. I use the spot meter to meter on middle gray (the shadows) and shoot. When you're stationary and the lighting conditions are stable, this is pretty easy to do.

The S110 contains a 12.1 megapixel CMOS image sensor. As a side benefit, it also shoots 1080p video which is crisp and clear. This little camera does very well in low light. I've shot a lot at night at ISO 3200 and have been happy with the results.

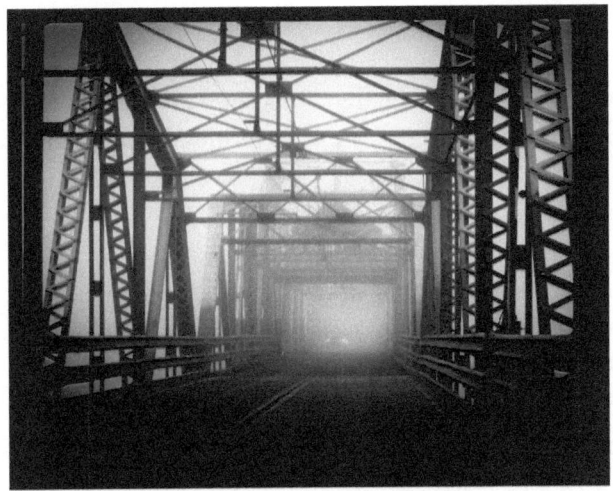

Grosse Ile Bridge, Grosse Ile, Michigan
Canon S110 f/4.5 at 1/250 ISO 1000

Canon G12 Setup

The G12 has a long standing, substantial cult following. I can see why. It's a hefty camera, but easy to shoot with and carry around. It's much smaller than a small DSLR. To me, the G12 lands somewhere between a DSLR and a point and shoot, since a lot of the controls are DSRL-like.

I think one of the big appeals of the Canon G series cameras are the external, manual controls. The mode selection is a dial that sits on top of the ISO dial. Exposure compensation is controlled by an easy to use dial on the left of the viewfinder. The LCD display is articulated, so that provides for a lot of good high and low positioned shots, especially if you're using a monopod. The exposure control (evaluative, center weighted and spot metering) is controlled by a button and the selection menu is instantly displayed.

I set up my G12 the same as my S110, using AV mode heavily and sometimes P mode. I'll switch between evaluative and spot metering depending where I am and the lighting conditions. I'll always default to evaluative metering. I also shoot in RAW for image quality.

The G12 shoots in RAW, which is a plus, but don't expect a fast cycle time between shots. A fast memory card helps this, but it's still on the slow side. As we know, RAW mode is simply data and can be considered a digital negative. There is a lot more data to write to the SD cards, so it takes a little longer. The alternative is to shoot in JPEG mode, but this limits your post-processing capabilities.

The G12 is a good camera with a good solid feel if you are not looking for really fast or sequential "decisive moment" street shots. It's great for environmental shots. The G12 contains a 10 megapixel CCD image sensor. It shoots 720p video which is outdated.

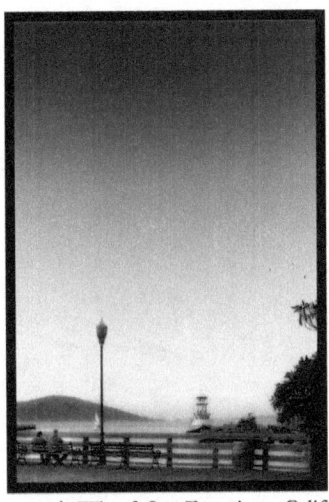

Fisherman's Wharf, San Francisco, California
Canon G12 f/2.8 at 1/200 ISO 640

Nikon S3100 Setup

For such an inexpensive camera, the Nikon S3100 (and S3600) has a lot of user settable features. You can set the white balance, ISO, autofocus area and mode along with other features. I set the white balance to auto and the ISO range to ISO Auto 800. This means the ISO will automatically adjust from ISO 80 to 800. You can adjust the ISO up to 3200 manually.

The Nikon S3100 contains a 20 megapixel CCD image sensor. It shoots 720p video which is outdated, like the G12.

The S3100 does not shoot in RAW, so I set it to 5152x3864 pixels, the highest resolution this camera offers. I set the autofocus (AF) mode to SF-S Single AF. The AF area mode offers five selections. I default mine to Target finding AF, but for shooting people walking subject tracking works well.

Another great feature of this little camera is the aperture and shutter speed display. Press the shutter release halfway down and the shutter speed and f-stop appear at the bottom of the LCD display. Discreetly setting the aperture and shutter speed are not available on this camera. You can change the ISO and that will change the shutter speed, but I have not experienced the camera changing the aperture. The only way to do this is to zoom in or out.

I don't worry too much about the lack of options and shooting modes with this camera. It's tiny, reliable and cycles reasonably fast with a good quality SD card. It produces solid shots you can work with.

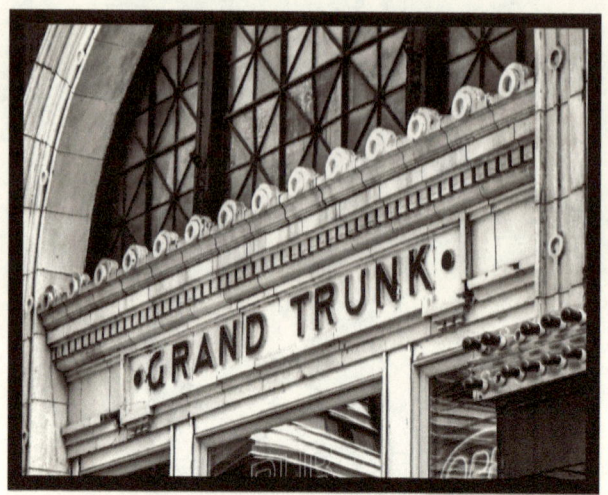

Grand Trunk, Detroit, Michigan
Nikon Coolpix S3100 f/6 at 1/60 ISO 400

Again, it really doesn't matter what type of point-and-shoot you use, since they all are pretty much the same. I find point-and-shoots easier to use and handle than smart phones since they're dedicated cameras. Plus, thieves are less prone to snatch a camera out of your hand than a smart phone (it used to happen a lot in downtown Detroit).

The more you learn about your camera and what it can and can't do, the easier it will be to shoot with and take great images.

Out In The Street

I like what Annie Liebovitz said in the book **Annie Liebovitz At Work**, *"The camera gave you a license to go out alone in the world with a purpose."* This observation is right on, and it's stuck with me. First, just go out and shoot on the streets. It doesn't have to be a major city or urban area. Small towns and cities offer many interesting and unusual shot opportunities. Smaller areas lack the indifference and anonymity of large cities, and you can work that to your advantage.

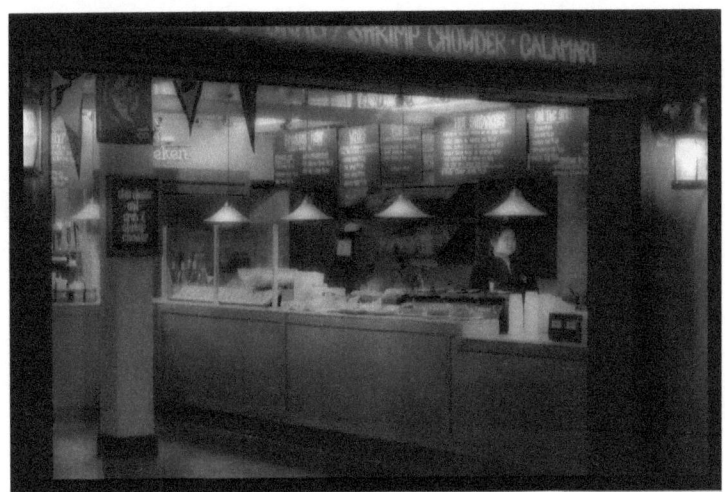

Fisherman's Wharf, San Francisco, California
Canon G12 f/5.6 at 1/60 ISO 640

As I mentioned earlier in this book about my lunchtime shoots, even if I only had a couple of good shots, at least I was *out there shooting*. The more you are in the street shooting, the more natural it becomes walking around with a camera and you will get better and better shots.

Pop-up Flash

Some well known street photographers, Bruce Gilden in particular, use flash a lot. It helps on the street even in bright daylight by highlighting your subject. Using flash puts an edge on your street photos, and if that's your style, go for it. Just set your flash to Auto or On and try it out.

Pop-up flash works really well at dusk and at night. If you're looking for New York City-ish type of nightlife shots, pop-up flash is the way to go. There are countless street fashion night shots that are taken with flash.

Moving vs. Stationary

Although there aren't really any rules in urban photography, there are generally two modes of operation- staying in one spot and waiting to see what passes by or walking around looking for shot opportunities. There are advantages to both.

I tend to stay in motion when I shoot. You cover more territory and there may be more opportunities to get good shots. Plus, it's less likely that you'll be approached by a street person if you're moving. You are much less visible in motion. It's hard to bother a moving target.

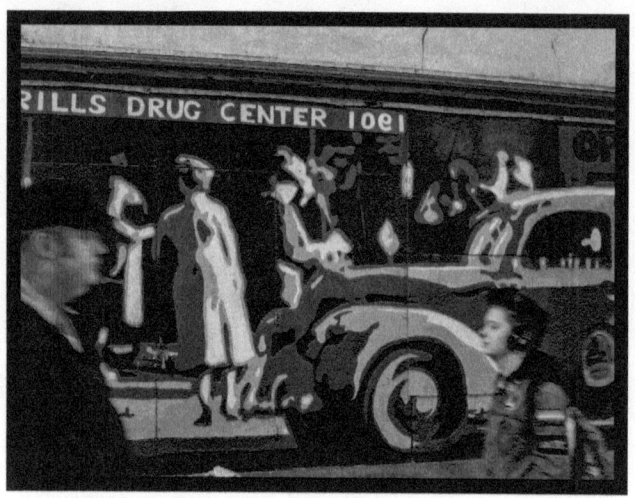

Market Street, San Francisco, California
Canon S110 f/3.5 at 1/50 ISO 3200

One technique with stationary urban photography is to find an interesting spot, especially with a unique background, and plant yourself. Sit on a bench facing the upstream flow of people. Steps of a building are even better, as long as there isn't a large flow of traffic. Don't hold your camera up constantly, focusing on and tracking people as they pass (unless you're taking shutter priority shots). This generally does two things- it puts people off or turns them on. They will either frown, scowl, or smile. Worse, they will look directly at the camera lens. Try and see your shot coming and take it quickly.

Go wide angle, for the most part, so have your lens zoomed all the way in. Find something above the flow of people that is unusual and is outside of the reality of everyday life. For example, large posters of fashion models who ooze privilege and wealth over street people wandering by is a good example. Find something that makes a statement about contemporary culture, like the Drug Center shot above.

Go telephoto after a few wide angle shots. This allows you to focus on groups or individuals and their interactions, facial expressions or intentions. Even with your lens zoomed all the way out, the depth of field, or how much is in focus, will probably be good. That's a characteristic of point and shoots for the most part. As an aside, cell phone cameras have infinite depth of field. Having a wide depth of field helps with urban photography. The background and surroundings will be in focus, giving the subject context.

On the other hand, if you want to isolate your subject by having it in focus and the background blurry, make sure you are in Aperture priority or Manual mode and use the lowest f-stop your camera allows.

People and Places

Urban photography is comprised of people and places, mostly in combination. A good day shooting is made up of interesting environmental shots, crowd shots and close ups of people of interest.

Here's an example. The two shots below were taken by the fountain on Belle Isle, an island park near downtown Detroit.

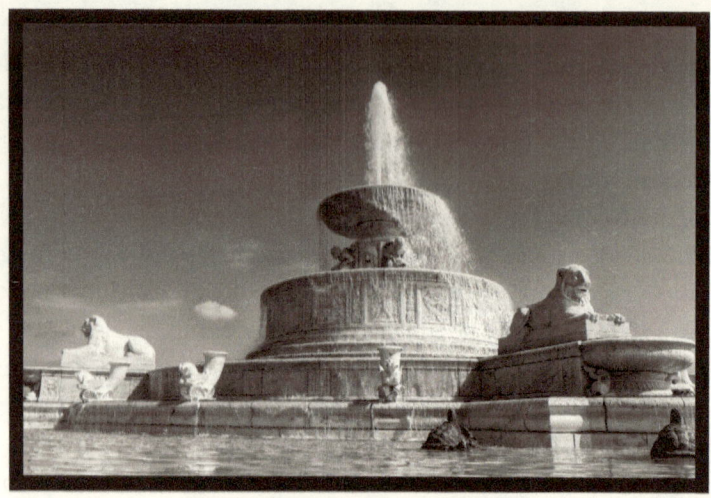

Belle Isle Fountain, Detroit, Michigan
Canon S110 f/8 at 1/1250 ISO 400

The image above is a well composed shot of the fountain with a deep sky, crisp whites and good shadow detail. It's *technically good*, but that's about it. Compare it to the shot below.

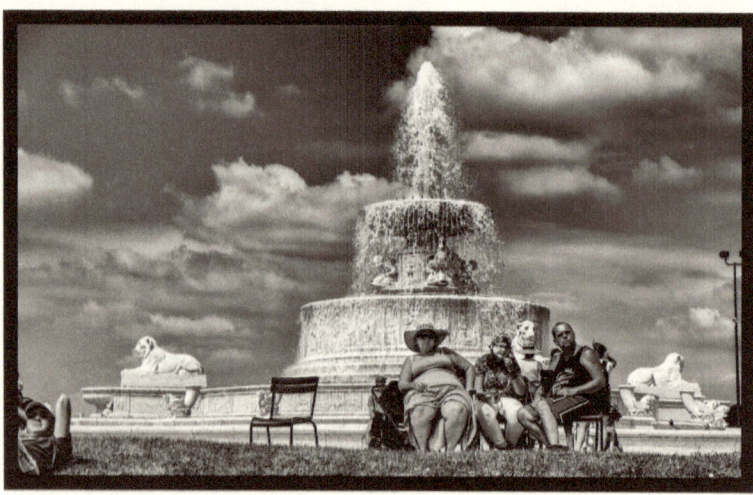

Belle Isle Fountain, Detroit, Michigan
Canon S110 f/8 at 1/1250 ISO 400

The interest goes up orders of magnitude when people are in the frame. Instead of a touristy or stock-photo type of shot, this image has subject and character, just by the inclusion of the cool eccentricity and individuality of the seated people.

Here's a shot that integrates people into an interesting environment. These men were eating lunch, checking out the urban graffiti that is vanishing with gentrification in this particular Detroit neighborhood. Did they notice me? Not at all. I was across the street, had my Nikon S3600 in my hand and got the shot on the fly. I probably stood still for five seconds or less when I took this.

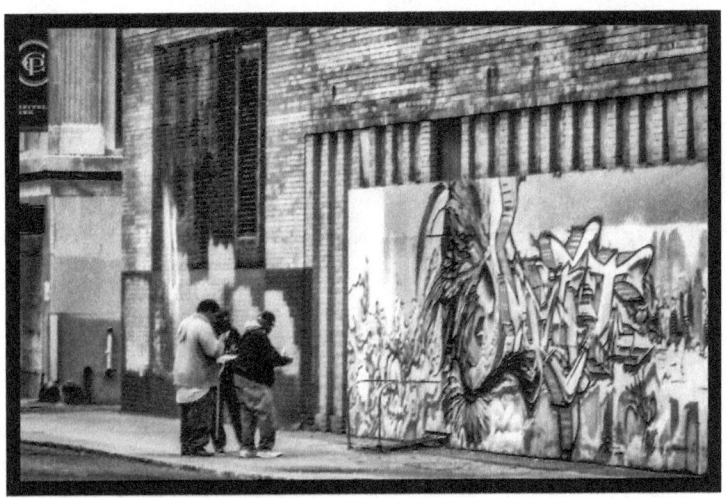

Capitol Park, downtown Detroit
Nikon S3600 f/6.5 at 1/80 ISO 80

There are shots like this all around you when you are out in the streets shooting. Just keep your eyes open. Also, look for themes and similarities in situations and environments. Sometimes basic truths will reveal themselves. The shot below is a woman looking at a painting at the Detroit Institute of Arts.

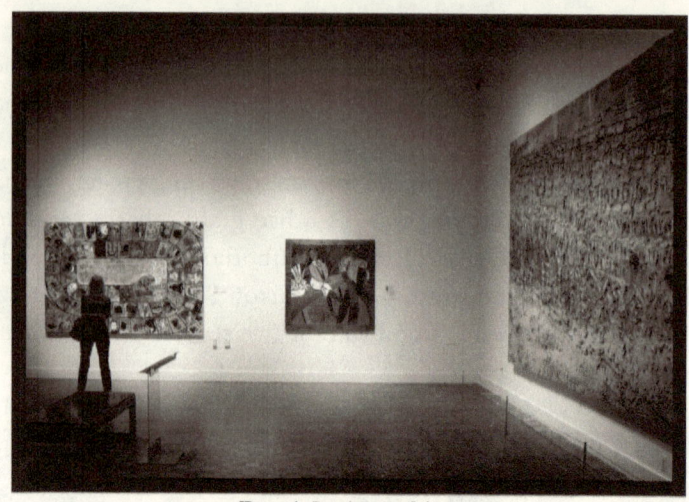

Detroit Institute of Arts
Canon G12 f/2.8 at 1/30 ISO 800

There is common ground between these two very diverse shots- people are fascinated by art no matter what the form or environment.

People

Of course people are everywhere in urban environments. Look for the interesting and unusual. I was struck by the woman and her suitcase stepping up onto the curb on her way to a bus station. Where was she going? She walked slowly, but confidently made her alone way down the street. Her jacket shined, and that caught my eye. Watching her, there was a sense of vulnerability but also confidence and tenacity in her steady progress. I had no doubt she would get where she was going.

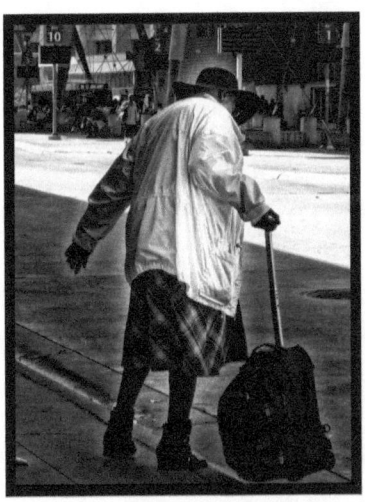

Traveler, Bus Station, downtown Detroit
Canon S110 f/5.9 at 1/400 ISO 400

The couple below were interesting, leaning in the shadows against the entrance to a dark parking structure. For me, there was a sense of mystery about this couple. The People Mover track above lends a sweeping diagonal line, framing the couple. If they weren't standing in the shadows, this would not have been an interesting shot.

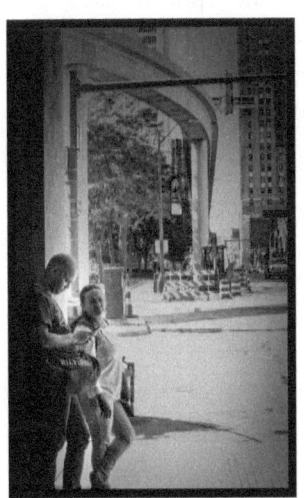

Couple, downtown Detroit
Canon S110 f/4.5 at 1/1250 ISO 400

This blind musician was playing at Detroit's Eastern Market, a large food and flea market. This is a study in trust and faith. He's played there for who knows how long and keeps the plastic cup in his jacket pocket for change from people passing by.

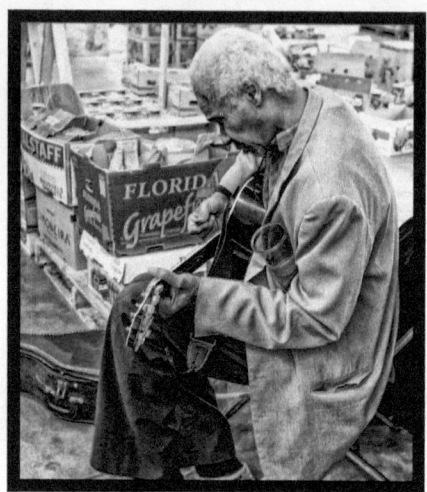

Musician, Eastern Market, Detroit
Canon S110 f/4.5 at 1/30 ISO 100

This woman walking on the opposite side of the street caught my eye, especially her position relative to the other two vertical objects, the fire hydrant and the light pole. The low concrete wall provided a good sweeping line across the bottom of the frame, while the black background provided solid negative space.

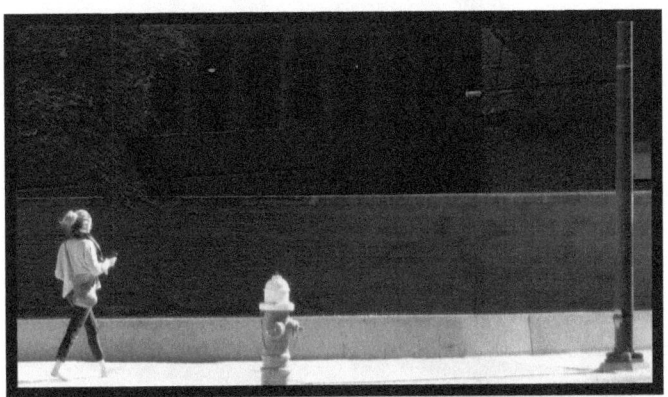

Woman Walking, downtown Detroit, Michigan
Canon S110 f/5.9 at 1/320 ISO 400

This woman strolling in the winter rain is offset by the shining, wet concrete was appealing to me. She was confident in her stride, even thought the Detroit Riverwalk was cold and deserted. The horizontal patterned umbrella contrasted well with the vertical, leafless trees.

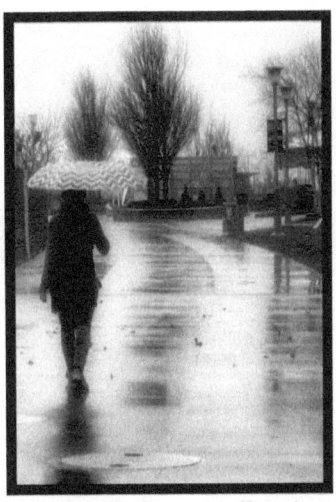

Riverwalk, downtown Detroit
Canon S110 f/5 at 1/640 ISO 500

Some people are very friendly toward the camera, like the man below. I asked him if I could take a couple of shots and he was happy to oblige and struck a couple of impromptu poses.

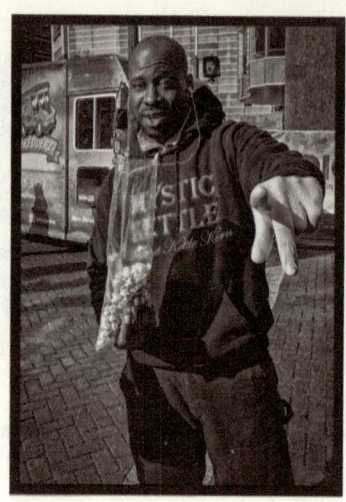

Popcorn Vendor, Campus Martius, downtown Detroit
Canon S110 f/11 at 1/250 ISO 400

This woman standing in the shadows selling popcorn is a good dark contrast to offset the light colored popcorn in the foreground. I really liked the way the light hit her face and features. It added drama to the shot.

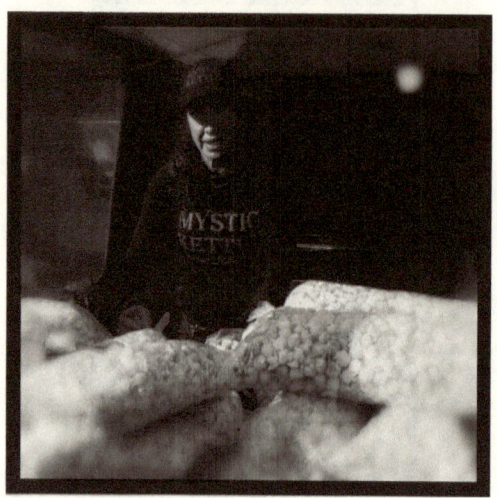

Popcorn Vendor, Campus Martius, downtown Detroit
Canon S110 f/11 at 1/100 ISO 400

These two generations of fishermen were happy to say hello as I took their picture as they walked by. As a rule in street photography, you do not talk to people and ask them to take a picture- you just shoot away. These people were different. The were friendly and we talked about what fish were running in the Detroit River at the moment. I asked to photograph them, and as you can see, they kindly cooperated.

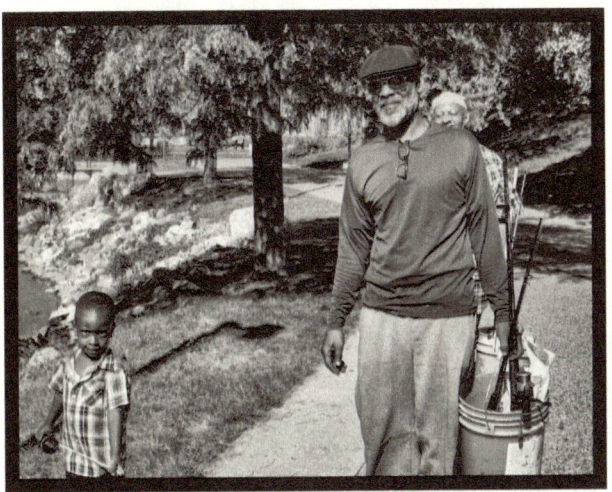

Fishermen, Riverwalk, Detroit, Michigan
Canon S110 f/8 at 1/1250 ISO 400

Try to get shots from parking structures and other elevated views. This isn't too difficult in an urban environment, and the results are usually good.

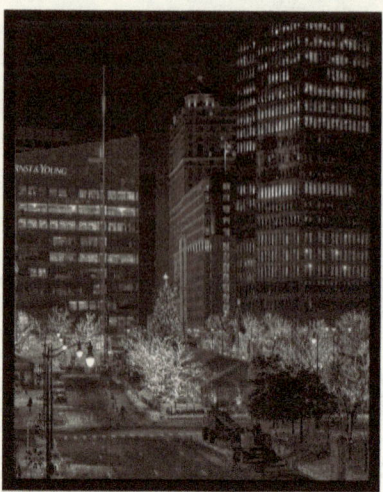

Campus Martius, Detroit, Michigan
Canon S110 f/5 at 1/30 ISO 1000

An Unusual Resource

Why do photographers like Diane Arbus and Robert Frank have such an impact on people? It's heart and pathos observing and capturing the human condition, I believe. Great urban photographs need to say something. Here's what I do to become more sensitive to the human condition. I read poetry. It sounds like apples and oranges- photography and poetry, but I see them as linked. What does a poet strive for? Images and emotions. We strive for the same thing. I like the hard core honesty of Charles Bukowski and C. K. Williams, the imagery of Amy Clampitt, and the clarity of Donald Justice, just to name a very few.

Check out a few contemporary poets. If anything you read moves you, work to translate that into an image. It's a giant step toward producing art.

Don't Get Overconfident

When you're shooting on the streets most people either ignore you or are friendly and obliging. Don't get over confident. The streets are volatile and sometimes unsafe. Just keep your eyes open and be aware of your surroundings and people near you. There's more about this in the Becoming Invisible chapter.

The Streets at Night

Night shooting takes on a personality of its own and adds drama to your shots. Your point-and-shoot should handle this well, with ISO values up to 12800 on some cameras. Yes, you will get grain in your images, but grain is good in urban photography.

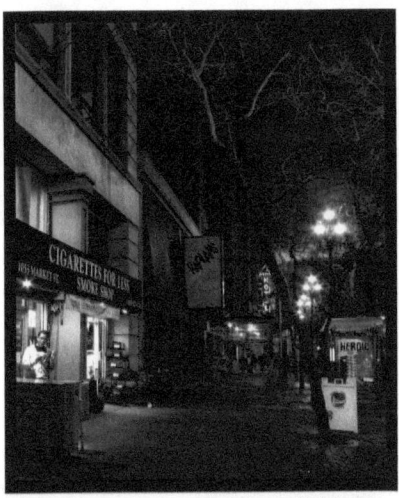

Market Street, San Francisco, California
Canon S110 f/4 at 1/60 ISO 1000

People seem different at night and the streets take on a new energy. Try and capture that in your images.

In the shot below, the people on the bus are interacting or absorbed in their own lives. Bus passengers provide a great cross-section of people and contemporary culture. It's no accident that the cover photograph of Robert Frank's **The Americans** are bus passengers.

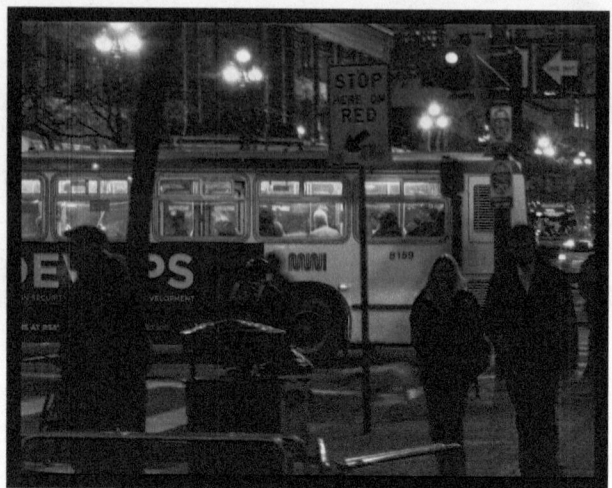

Market Street, San Francisco, California
Canon S110 f/5.9 at 1/8 ISO 1000

I took these shots on Market Street in San Francisco. Market Street sparkles with life at night and there's always a diverse crowd to shoot. The lighting is great, so it's hard to miss a good shot.

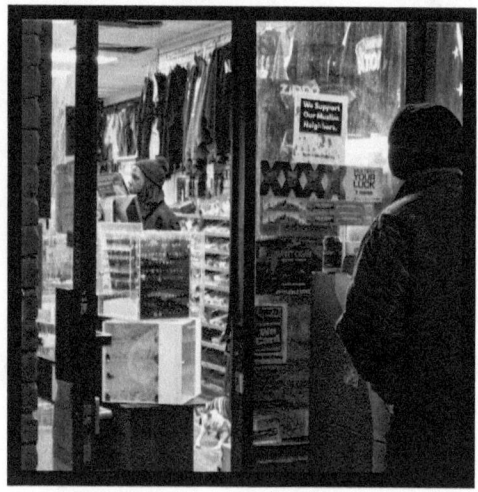

Market Street, San Francisco, California
Canon S110 f/5.9 at 1/8 ISO 1000

Again, shooting on the street is mostly about people. Here I focused on storefront and vendors hawking their wares on the sidewalk.

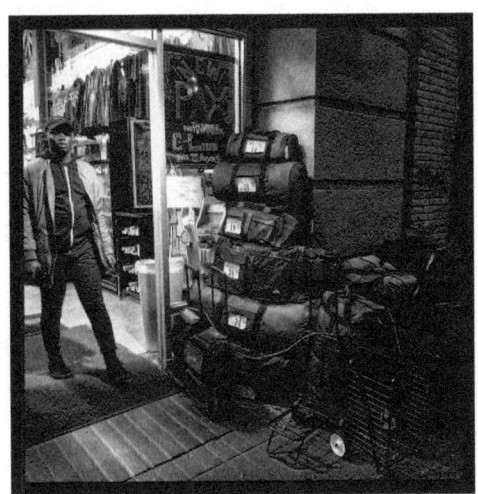

Market Street, San Francisco, California
Canon S110 f/5.9 at 1/8 ISO 1000

Every city has a street that comes alive at night. Photography yours during the day and at night. Check out your main drag, pick a spot and shoot what moves along. Look for leading lines that accentuate your shot and good lighting contrast.

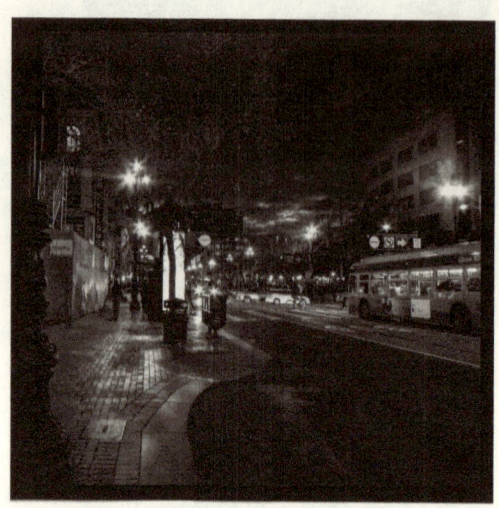

Market Street, San Francisco, California
Canon S110 f/4 at 1/60 ISO 3200

Look for pavement reflections and streetlights and don't be afraid to crank up your ISO. Don't worry about grain. I actually like it, and I like the natural star effect on the streetlights. Try and keep the shutter speed above 1/30 of a second, otherwise your images will blur. Built in image stabilization helps, but it only goes so far.

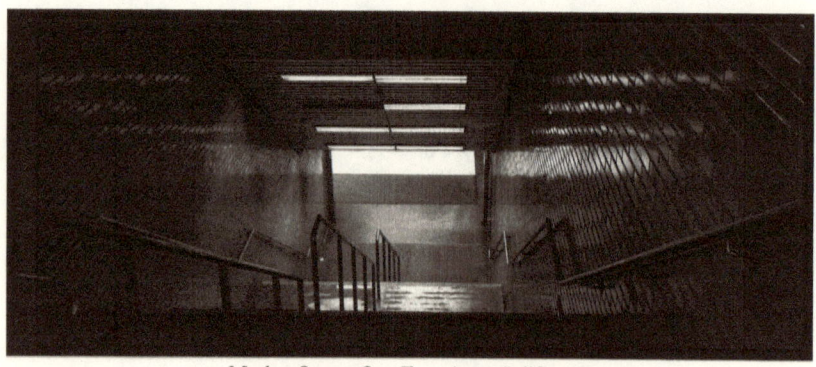

Market Street, San Francisco, California
Canon S110 f/4 at 1/2100 ISO 3200

If you can, steady your camera on something, like a ledge or bench. Some photographers use a monopod to shoot. This has its advantages and disadvantages. It certainly stabilizes your shots and you can use it to get elevated or pavement level shots easily. On the down side, it handicaps your shots and makes you much more conspicuous. If you repeatedly go back to an active street to shoot, use a monopod on one of your outings to shoot the environment at night, just to try it out. Shoot low and high. You will have a robust portfolio of your outings over time- people, culture and environment, all the basic components of quality urban photography.

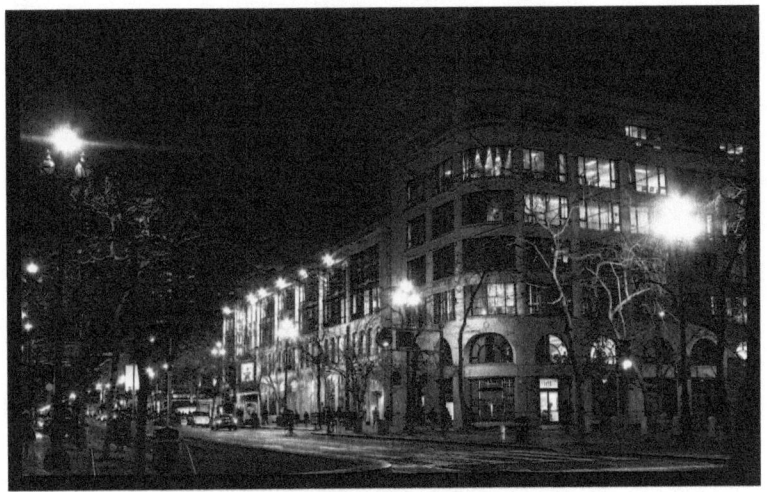

Market Street, San Francisco, California
Canon S110 f/3.5 at 1/80 ISO 3200

Histograms

Some of this text appeared in the **DSLR Artist II**, but it needs to be repeated here because it's so important, especially for night photography.

A histogram provides exposure information, laid out on an X (horizontal) and Y (vertical) axis. The horizontal X axis is measured in units of brightness, with pure black on the extreme left and pure white on the extreme right. The vertical Y axis is measured in pixel units.

Histograms look somewhat like bell curves. For a "correct" exposure more pixels are in the midrange than those on the left or right. I put correct in quotes because there is really no correct exposure. You may want to have areas blown out (excessive white) or with deep, black shadows (excessive black). Even when striving for these effects, starting in the middle from an optimal overall exposure is a good idea. It gives you a baseline to work from.

Histograms are easy to get to. I press the playback button then the display button to bring up the image on the LCD display. I then press the display button again or info button and the brightness histogram appears adjacent to the image, along with other exposure information. If I press the display button again or info button the RGB histogram appears along with all the other data. The RGB histogram provides exposure information for the red, green and blue channels. For example, if you're taking photos of a deep green jungle, then the green channel will be more dense than the red and blue. Histograms are very easy to read and give you an instant exposure sanity check. This works the same on most cameras.

The figure below is a schematic representation of the LCD display on the back of a DSLR. I hand drew the images and did not photograph actual LCD display histograms since it's hard to just concentrate on the histogram due to all the other information presented.

Like stated above, there are buttons you press when cycling through an image displayed on you camera's LCD. You will eventually come to a display that show the image, its histogram and other exposure information such as the image size, the date it was taken, ISO, aperture and the like.

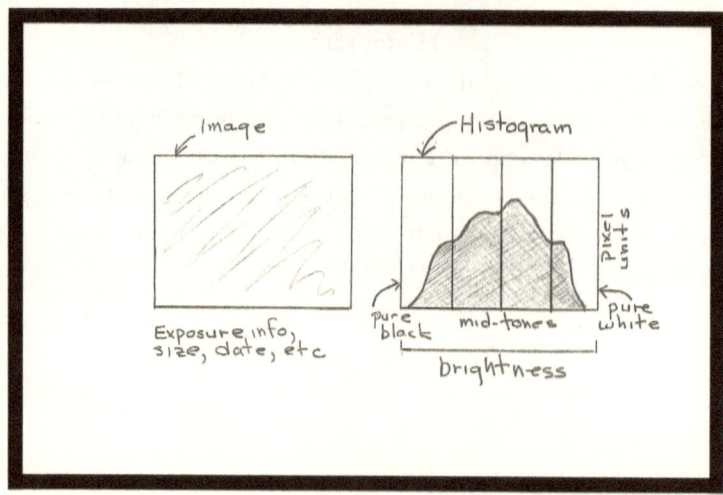

"Proper" Exposure

Proper is in quotes since there really is no "proper" exposure. You may want a lot of black or the highlights being blown out in an image. All proper means is that most of the exposure is in the mid-tones and no information in the image is lost. The pure black and pure white edges will not be touched by the pixel values. Most of the pixels will be distributed around the center, as shown below. There will be spikes here and there, for sure, but the pixels will still tend toward the middle.

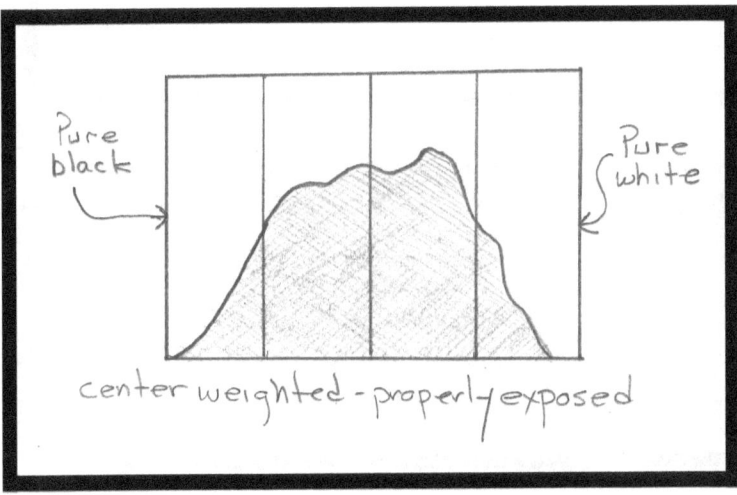

Underexposure

If an image is underexposed, the pixels will be skewed to the left toward pure black.

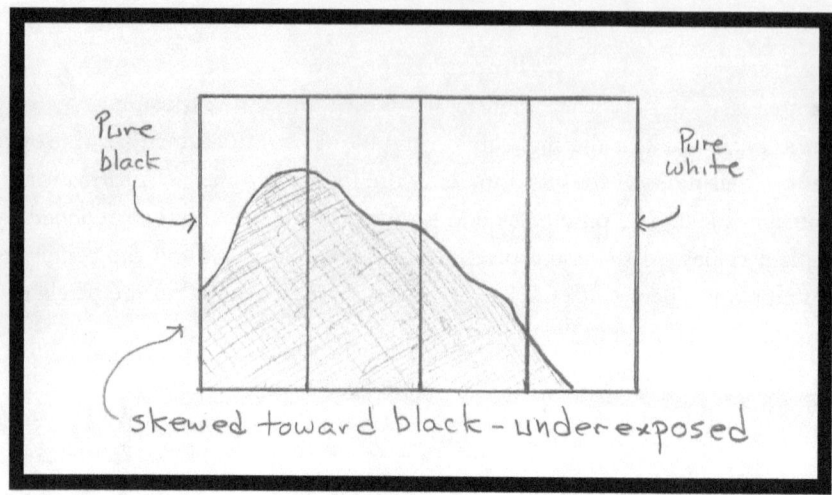

skewed toward black - underexposed

If this isn't what you want, you will need to increase the exposure by opening up the lens aperture, decrease the shutter speed or increase the ISO setting.

Overexposure

If an image is overexposed, the pixels with be skewed to the right toward pure white.

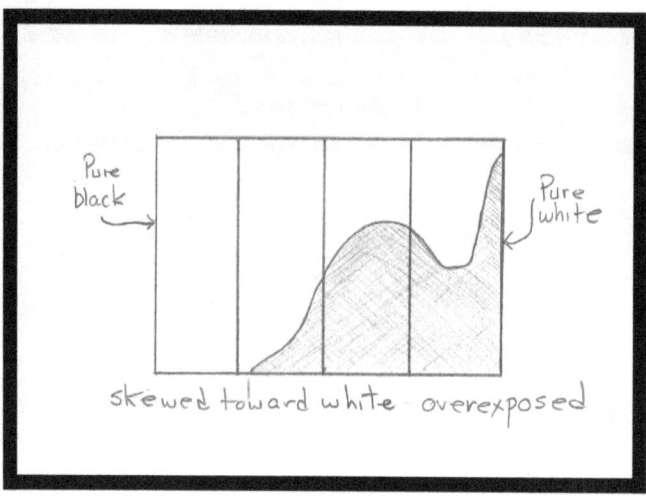

skewed toward white overexposed

In terms of information loss, this is worse than underexposure. If this is not what you want, then you need to decrease the exposure by setting a larger f-stop on your lens, increase the shutter speed or decrease the ISO setting. Don't always expect your histogram to look like a nice, clean bell curve. In many situations it won't. If you're shooting in a high contrast environment, then you may have two spikes near both ends of your histogram. Here's where checking the histogram really comes in handy. If you have a spike on the left side of the histogram then you have lost most, if not all, shadow detail. If that's what you want, then okay. If not you will have to increase your exposure. If there's a spike on the right side, then most if not all of the highlight detail is lost and you will need to decrease exposure.

Beware of Your LCD Display

Do not depend on an image display alone on your camera's LCD to determine proper exposure. The LCD display is affected by the lighting conditions you are shooting in. The histogram is always consistent. Use that.

Again, it is better to be a tad underexposed than overexposed. Why? There is total information loss when an image is overexposed. Pure white is pure white and no information can be recovered by post processing. Areas of the image will be "blown out", meaning pure white. Sometimes this is a good thing if you are taking a high key portrait or shot of an object. You may want the background close to pure white but not your subject.

Unless your image is grossly underexposed, a lot of the underexposed pixels can be brightened by increasing the exposure in post processing. I like to underexpose my shots by at least a half a stop and, if necessary, increase the exposure during post processing, usually in Lightroom.

Again, don't be afraid to crank up your ISO at night and try not to shoot under 1/30 of a second. Do the best to stabilize your shots and you'll wind up with great images.

Becoming Invisible

The biggest fear, and biggest risk in street photography is having someone come after you when you're shooting. Most people could care less and ignore you. When I first starting shooting on the streets, I thought everyone would stare and possibly approach me. The opposite is true. Almost everyone pays you no mind at all. Why should they? People are engrossed in their own lives and thoughts. If they're walking the streets they more than likely have somewhere to go and are focused on getting there and not on you. Just try and stay out of the way. Don't block a sidewalk or intersection while you compose a shot. That's all part of being invisible.

Keep Quiet

Do not draw attention to yourself or your camera. That's why point-and-shoots are great urban cameras. First, make sure your camera doesn't make any noise. Most digital cameras have sound control. Make sure all sound is off. No beeps, no bells. Second, give people their personal space. If a photographer came up to me and shot inches from my nose with a flash, I wouldn't be very happy. These are the times we live in: people can be angry and volatile. Do not provoke them.

Wear Black

Wear dark colored clothes, preferably black. This is generally a photographer's uniform. I usually wear a black t-shirt and black or blue jeans or dark cargo pants when I shoot. I'll wear a dark coat or jacket in Winter. Dark clothes seem to blend you into the environment easily.

Shoot From the Hip with No Eye Contact

The second important thing is to not make eye contact with the people you are trying to shoot. Pretend you are looking beyond them and taking a photo of something else.

You can also "shoot from the hip", although this takes a little practice. If you're sitting on a bench, take an hour or so to shoot people passing by with the camera in your lap or to the side. Some people may notice, most will not. Over time you will get the feel of where to aim your camera to get the shots you want. This works well when you're riding in a bus or subway.

All of this isn't being sneaky or dishonest. On the contrary, you want natural, candid, non-contrived shots. Having people not noticing you is your biggest asset when shooting in the streets.

What if You're Hassled?

What if someone comes after you? First, walk away. If they follow and get in your face, just tell them you were shooting something else and say you're sorry. Most people will accept this. Be friendly. If they really hassle you and ask for your camera and get physical, make sure you have an "out", such as ducking into a store or other crowded place. This is very rare and will probably not happen, but always be prepared for the worst.

This text appeared in the **Medium Format Film Photography** book, but I'm repeating it here, since it's so relevant to urban photography.

So, can you get into hot water legally photographing people? It depends where you live. Firstly, I'm not a lawyer but this is what I understand. In the United States, you can photograph who and what you want in public places, or in places where photography is allowed. This means you can shoot on the streets with no issues. Regarding private property, you need permission to shoot inside or on the property, but you may photograph the property from a public place. You can also shoot the general population, accidents, fires, children, celebrities, law enforcement officers, criminal activities and arrests. You do not have to explain what you are doing to anyone, including police officers, but just make sure you are not obstructing public officials in the discharge of their duties. No one can take your camera equipment or images without a warrant.

So what about publishing photographs with people in it? Again, from my understanding, if you are not using a likeness of a person to promote a product, service, idea or thing, or to disparage the person, a model release is not required. Again, I'm no lawyer so do not take what I say for gospel, but I believe that applies to the type of photographs this book conveys. We're producing artistic urban photographs, not opinions or advertisements for products or services.

Processing Your Images

I use Adobe Lightroom for most of my image processing. There are other many other programs available, such as Pixelmator for the Mac and GIMP, which is open source and is free. Pixelmator and GIMP are photoshop competitors. They are both fine programs. Pixelmator at the time of this writing is $30, which is more than reasonable. There's a "pro" version also on the market. Pixelmator is only available for Macintosh computers. GIMP works for both PCs and Macs.

Although I have and use Photoshop, I work in Lightroom almost all the time, especially with urban images. I mostly use it to convert from color to black and white and to enhance my shots.

Lightroom Example Walkthrough

Here's an example walkthrough of an urban color image converted to black and white and enhanced in Lightroom. This shot was taken at Campus Martius, downtown Detroit in the summer.

The image adjustment controls are all on the right. Make sure all of the Tone and Presence sliders are set to zero. The next step is to simply click from Color to Black and White, as shown below.

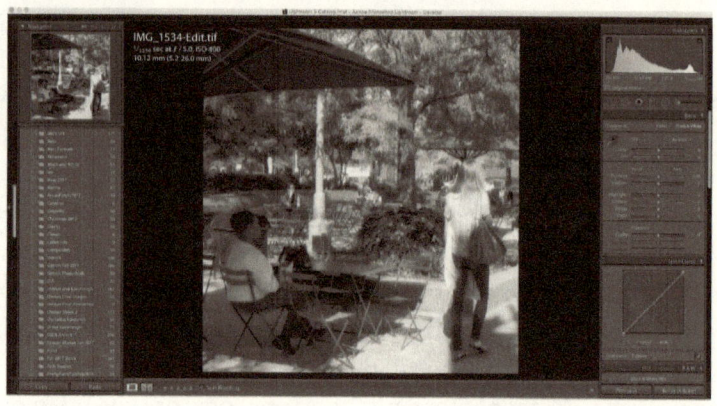

This turns the image to monochrome. There is a lot of middle gray in this image and it's low contrast. All we really need to do now is play with the Tone and Presence sliders. The Tone controls are Exposure, Contrast, Highlights, Shadows, Whites and Blacks. The Presence controls are Clarity, Vibrance and Saturation.

The exposure looks okay to the eye and by the histogram in the upper right corner. It's weighted toward the black end and so is the image. The dark areas are on the left. We want this image to have more contrast and more shadow detail. To increase the contrast, bump up the contrast slider very slightly, around +15. The contrast slider changes the contrast of the entire image. I tend to avoid overusing the contrast control. Contrast is really the difference between black and white, so I first adjust the black and white sliders. I tend to like bright whites and dark blacks. I then adjust the shadow and highlight sliders. Here is the final image in Lightroom before exporting it as a JPEG.

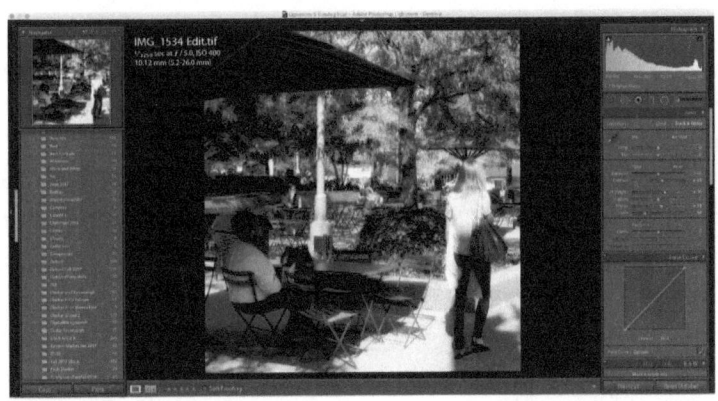

As you can see the image contains more contrast, brighter whites and deeper blacks with decent shadow detail. This only takes a few minutes to adjust and can take a muddy image to one with good contrast in just a few steps. It takes practically no time to adjust and enhance an image once you get the hang of it.

I sometimes adjust the image using the Clarity slider. This makes an image softer or harsher and is one of the better tools in Lightroom. The image above was already soft, so I kept the Clarity at zero.

Getting Your Work Seen

Getting your work seen is easy and doesn't really cost anything except time and effort. First, build a website or blog highlighting your work. There are many free hosting sites available. I use Wordpress, which is one of many. Why? My first site used Wordpress, so I'm familiar with it. There are many free and good looking templates available that will make your photos look first class.

Also, if you're inclined and like to write, include a blog. Write about your shoots, your cameras, your technique- whatever comes to mind. After your website is up and you have blog posts ready to go, how will people know about you? That's where social media comes into play. I'm on Twitter and occasionally use Facebook, but that's about it. I like Twitter because I can follow other photographers and artists whose work I like.

If you're genuinely interested in your art and are not pushing or trying to sell your work, you will get a lot of Twitter followers. Nothing is more of a turn off than a bloated ego trying to sell their images and celebritize themselves. Let your work stand on its own, and don't pretend to be something or somebody you're not. Also, if you admire someone's work, let them know by hitting the Like button.

When you publish a blog post, make sure your categories are correct and you have a lot of tags. This helps people find your work. Add links to your social media outlets so when your page is published, your friends and followers are notified.

Start a YouTube channel. It's easier than you think. Use a smart phone for video if that's all you have, but your point-and-shoot might shoot video in 1080p. Document your shoots. Create reviews. Show people your cameras and talk about them. Don't worry if your videos are not perfect- nobody's are. Maintain a good level of quality and keep the content slanted toward your target group: urban photographers just like you. Keep the content flow on a reasonable cadence, such as one new video a week or two and people will watch and subscribe to your channel.

Learn from others, especially other artists whose work exceeds yours. It's human to be envious of others, but turn that envy into admiration and aspiration. You will be a better photographer, and better person for it.

Great Street Photographers

There are too many great street photographers to list here, but these are the individuals that I admire, respect and have influenced my work.

Henri Cartier-Bresson

Henri Cartier-Bresson was born in France in 1908. Cartier-Bresson started out as a painter then was drawn to a photographic surrealist movement emerging in France. He was one of the founders of Magnum Photos, of which W Eugene Smith was associated with much later.

Cartier-Bresson shot with a Leica 35mm rangefinder with a 50mm lens, and not much more.

Why I Like Cartier-Bresson

The first time I saw a Cartier-Bresson was at the Detroit Institute of Arts. The photograph was Hyeres, France, 1932. I stared at it for about fifteen minutes, wandered around the museum, then came back to it twice. It's one of my all time favorite photographs, how the stairs spiral down to the man speeding on the bicycle. Cartier-Bresson is a master of instantaneous composition, and we as photographers can learn a great deal from him. Armed with a simple 35mm rangefinder and a 50mm lens, not much more is needed to produce great art, which is a great lesson to photographers. Henri Cartier-Bresson died in 2004 in France.

Outstanding Photographs
Hyères, France, 1932
Nehru Announces Gandhi's Death
Sumatra, Indonesia, 1952
To Tell the Truth, New York, 1959

Bruce Gilden

Bruce Gilden is the most brazen street photographer I've seen. He works the streets fearlessly, getting right in people's faces firing a flash. His work is featured in museums from Tokyo to London. Born in 1946, Gilden is still shooting. Gilden uses a Leica with a tethered flash unit. One of Gilden's well know quotes is, "If you can smell the street by looking at a photo, it must be street photography."

Why I Like Bruce Gilden

Gilden's fearlessness is so impressive, the way he gets inches from a person's face and fires away with his flash. I'm no shrinking violet, but this is something I doubt if I could do. His images are unmistakable and instantly recognizable.

Outstanding Photographs

These are not so much individual photographs, but collections and projects. Check out:

American Made
Women Casino Workers
Tough Guys
Moscow

Garry Winograd

Garry Winograd shot over five million photographs. I read that he left behind over 2,500 rolls of undeveloped film, three times as many developed rolls, and thousands of contact sheets that he never saw. Garry Winograd was possibly the most prolific street photographer of all time. Winograd was born in 1928 and grew up in the Bronx. He studied painting and photography and primarily shot in New York City. Winograd died in Tijuana Mexico in 1984. He shot mostly in the 1950s up until the early 1980s.

Why I Like Garry Winograd

Garry Winograd seemed to capture the street energy of New York City like no other photographer.

Outstanding Photographs

Like most urban photographers, Winograd's photographs are not named and a lot appear in collections. The J Paul Getty Museum houses many of Winograd's photographs, and some are named.

Untitled, American, 1964

World's Fair, New York City, American, 1964

Hollywood and Vine, Los Angeles, American, 1969

Texas, American, 1964

American Legion Convention, Dallas, American, 1964

Lee Friedlander

Lee Friedlander didn't just shoot people. He shot the environment of his time. Born in Washington in 1934, he attended art school in Pasadena, California then moved to New York City. Friedlander was another Leica rangefinder user and shot in black and white.

Why I Like Lee Friedlander

Friedlander started out photographing jazz musicians early in his career. To me, these are his best photographs, especially the images captured in after hours clubs. He also photographed strange, almost absurdist juxtapositions of objects and people that captured his time.

Outstanding Photographs

It's best to look at Lee Friedlander's portfolios, such as:

The Street

At Work

American Musicians

America by Car

Robert Frank

Robert Frank, best known for the book The Americans, was born in in Switzerland in 1924. He emigrated to the United States in 1947 where he shot fashion for Harpers Bazaar. During the many road trips Frank took he shot around 28,000 exposures. Frank used a Leica rangefinder along with 35, 50, and 90mm lenses. From pre-teen Lolitas with dangling cigarettes from their lips to starlets at Hollywood movie premiers to working class lunch counters in Detroit, Robert Frank captured America and its diverse, arid everyday life.

Why I Like Robert Frank

There's a rawness about Frank's work, and an uncanny ability to capture cultural and economic diversity in a single image. Frank lacks the prurience of Diane Arbus and is more objective, which I believe give his images a wider appeal. Each Robert Frank image sends a message, and it's not always good.

Outstanding Photographs
Butte, Montana, 1955
Parade, Hoboken, New Jersey 1955
Indianapolis, 1956
Sagamore Cafeteria, NYC, 1954

Vivian Maier

If there is ever an enigmatic photographer, it's Vivian Maier, born in 1926. Working as a nanny the bulk of her life, Maier shot in the streets with a Rolliflex TLR on her days off, capturing people and places. Maier was unknown until 1978 when a man named John Maloof bought 30,000 of her photographs for four hundred dollars. Once published, Maier has become a street photography sensation, and for good reason. Her work is incredible.

As far as I know, Maier used a medium format Rolliflex TLR (Twin Lens Reflex) camera. Maier shot mainly on the streets of New York City and Chicago. Impoverished, Maier died in 2009 in relative obscurity.

Why I Like Vivian Maier

Vivian Maier was driven, shooting a hundred thousand rolls of medium format film. She shot constantly on her days off as a nanny. This to me is the hallmark of a true artist. I believe Vivian Maier shot in the streets not because she wanted to, but was compelled to by some inner force.

Outstanding Photographs

Since Vivian Maier was virtually unknown as a photographer, her photographs aren't named as far as I can tell. The best data there is are dates for her photographs, and those can be sparse. On the Vivian Maier website there are several galleries to look through, all filled with great street photography.

Again, these are just of few of the significant urban and street photographers. Running the risk of sounding cliched, they were true trailblazers and you can do nothing but benefit from studying their work.

Final Thoughts

Develop your eye. For most people, photography is simply pressing a button, but not for urban photographers. Henri Cartier-Bresson said, *"That which must be learned cannot be taught."* It makes sense. Anyone can press a shutter button. Artists practice their craft, continuously. You learn, discover and grow as a photographer with practice.

Practice shooting using a few composition examples in this book and your eye will develop. Don't sit around and think about shooting, *go out and do it.* Shoot when the weather's bad. Shoot when it's cold. Shoot when it's too hot.

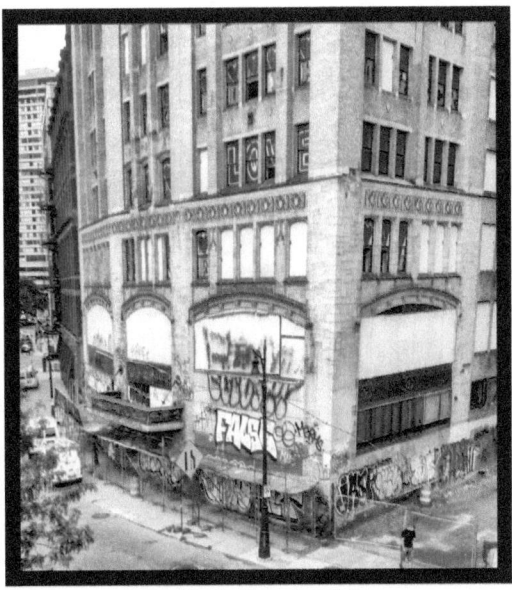

Capitol Park, Detroit, Michigan
iPhone 4S
f/2.4 at 1/280

Remember Garry Winograd and how he took over five million photographs? Did he think about going out and shooting? No. He just did it. Start accumulating images. Shoot every day. It's no hassle carrying around a small point and shoot. After shooting everyday for awhile, if you are out in the street shooting and don't have your camera you'll feel like something is missing, like forgetting your cell phone. Your small camera becomes part of you, and you become part of the streets.

Notes

Notes

Notes

Notes

Notes

About the Author

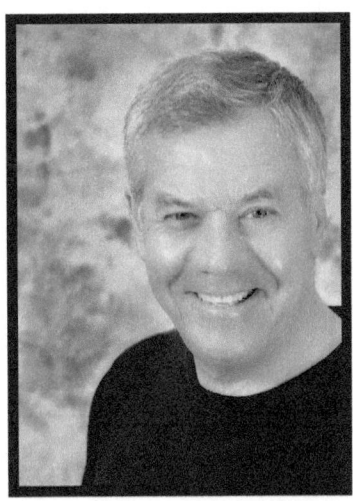

Jeff Stefan is the principle photographer and videographer at **J Stefan Photography**, based in Southeastern Michigan. Jeff is the author of **Medium Format Photography, Exploiting Your Point and Shoot, The Essentials of 35mm Film Photography** and **The DSLR Artist,** all available on Amazon.com.